CHURCH AND STATE
CHANGING PARADIGMS
Monsignor W. Onclin Chair 1999

KATHOLIEKE UNIVERSITEIT LEUVEN
Faculteit Kerkelijk Recht
Faculty of Canon Law

# CHURCH AND STATE
# CHANGING PARADIGMS

Monsignor W. Onclin Chair 1999

UITGEVERIJ PEETERS
LEUVEN
1999

C.I.P. Koninklijke Bibliotheek Albert I

ISBN 90-429-0749-5
D.1999/0602/38

© 1999 Uitgeverij Peeters, Bondgenotenlaan 153, B-3000 Leuven (Belgium)

# INHOUDSTAFEL / TABLE OF CONTENTS

R. TORFS, Crisis in het kerkelijk recht . . . . . . . . . . . . . . . 7

R. TORFS, Crisis in Canon Law . . . . . . . . . . . . . . . . . . 19

C. MIGLIORE, Ways and Means of the International Activity of the
Holy See . . . . . . . . . . . . . . . . . . . . . . . . . . . . 31

J.E. WOOD, The Role of Religion in the Advancement of Religious
Human Rights . . . . . . . . . . . . . . . . . . . . . . . . . 43

Personalia . . . . . . . . . . . . . . . . . . . . . . . . . . . . 71

Publicaties / Publications Msgr. W. Onclin Chair . . . . . . . . . 73

# CRISIS IN HET KERKELIJK RECHT

R. Torfs

## CRISIS?

Is er sprake van een crisis in het kerkelijk recht? Alvast niet voor wie naar het aantal opleidingen kijkt. Er komen er voortdurend bij: Boedapest, Mexico-Stad, Rome, Yaoundé[1]. Bovendien zijn kerkelijke wetgevers behoorlijk actief en tonen de media een levendige belangstelling voor recht in de kerk. En toch is niet alles rozengeur en maneschijn. Waar het canoniek recht als discipline staat, is hoe langer hoe minder duidelijk, en discussies erover zijn wat afgenomen in vergelijking met enkele decennia terug[2]. En hoewel er dus meer opleidingen dan ooit zijn, telt men minder grote canonisten, minder mensen die zowat als een *landmark* in hun vakgebied fungeren, die kunnen worden bijgetreden of afgevallen, maar die alleszins heel duidelijk bestaan. Nu verdient een stelling als de laatste wel enige scepsis. Grote canonisten overlijden wel[3], maar worden niet geboren: zij melden zich hoogstens langzaam aan na een jarenlang groeiproces. Maar toch, ondanks deze poging tot troost, er is een zekere schaarste. Kortom, tegenover meer opleidingen, meer wetgeving en meer mediabelangstelling, staan minder intellectuele debatten en minder markante canonisten. Wijst dat op een crisis? Minstens op een dalletje, vrees ik. Hoe zou dat komen? Ik zou daarover een persoonlijke visie willen geven, die subjectief is, of toch niet objectief in de klassieke zin, dus niet afstandelijk en onbevooroordeeld. Deze subjectieve aanpak betekent meteen dat ik vanuit een West-Europees standpunt schrijf, een andere keuze is er nu eenmaal niet, en dat ik bedank voor een cultuur-pessimistisch verklaringsmodel, gekenmerkt door uithalen naar het narcisme, individualisme en egoïsme van de moderne mens, want ik ben er zelf één, vooral dan wat de negatieve aspecten betreft.

---

[1] Boedapest, 30 november 1996; Mexico-Stad, 4 september 1995; Rome, Ateneo Romano della Santa Croce, 28 maart 1993; Yaoundé, 15 november 1991.

[2] S. Berlingò, *L'ultimo diritto. Tensioni escatologiche nell'ordine dei sistemi*, Turijn, G. Giappichelli, 1998, 258 p.

[3] E. Corecco (1931 - 1995), P. Gismondi (†1986), P.A. d'Avack (†1982), P. Lombardía (1930 - 1986), W. Onclin (1905 - 1989), P. Huizing (1911 - 1995).

De crisis van het canoniek recht – of het dalletje – kan wellicht worden verklaard aan de hand van drie momentopnamen in het kerkelijk recht, namelijk een beeld van het wetboek van 1917, van dat van 1983, en tenslotte een gezondheidsrapport bij aanvang van het jaar 1999, wat bangelijk op het randje van weer eens een millennium, want ze vliegen toch zo snel voorbij, onze millennia.

## EERSTE MOMENTOPNAME: HET KERKELIJK WETBOEK VAN 1917

Het kerkelijk wetboek van 1917, een pareltje van Pietro Gasparri, is een oorlogskind. Het kwam tot stand tijdens de eerste wereldoorlog, op een belangrijke breuklijn van de geschiedenis. Europa verkwanselde toen schijnbaar vrijwillig zijn eigen hegemonie. De democratisering van de samenleving stond voor de deur. Een vreemde aarzeling hing in lucht: twijfel tussen mistroostige lankmoedigheid en nieuwe durf. De sfeer van *De toverberg* van Thomas Mann. Dus een mooi moment voor een wetboek. Gasparri loste daarbij de verwachtingen in. Hij leverde een harmonieus werkstuk af. Het wetboek reflecteerde de kerk van die tijd, een hiërarchische priesterkerk waarin bijvoorbeeld de positie van de leek nauwelijks aan de orde was. Die vroeg daar trouwens ook niet zo om. Onder de vijf boeken van de Codex viel vooral het boek *De rebus* op. Het zakenrecht bevatte liefst 826 van de 2414 canones. Het hele sacramentenrecht werd tot het zakenrecht gerekend. Voor theologen en commentatoren, later, in de jaren zestig en zeventig was dat een vloek. Hoe kunnen sacramenten met hun theologische rijkdom in godsnaam deel uitmaken van het zakenrecht, die nuchtere, civielrechtelijke discipline die eigendom en vruchtgebruik beschrijft, erfpacht en opstal? Ofschoon verontwaardiging best voorzichtig wordt tegemoet getreden, is de oude plaatsbepaling toch niet onbegrijpelijk. Vooreerst was in 1917, zoals in de grote codificaties van de negentiende eeuw, het zakenrecht, draaiend rondom de blijvende waarde van het onroerend goed, hoeksteen van de rurale samenleving, nog steeds zowat de rechtstak bij uitstek. Wat waardevol was, genoot bescherming in het zakenrecht. De sacramenten zaten er dus goed. Bovendien biedt een zakenrechtelijke situering aan sacramenten de grootst mogelijke helderheid. Statische helderheid, dat zeker, maar helderheid. De sacramenten staan als een huis. Ook letterlijk. De milde zekerheid van onroerend goed.

Eigenlijk is de Codex van 1917 een consequente uitwerking van de *societas perfecta*-leer. Voor wie kerkelijk is, is de kerk een geheel eigen maatschappij zoals een andere. Ze staat niet zomaar in de maatschappij, ze is er zelf één. Met haar eigen recht, waarin sacramenten even reële dingen zijn als huizen in de profane samenleving van de negentiende en vroege twintigste eeuw. Slechts wanneer eigendom diefstal wordt, kan een sacrament geen zaak meer zijn. Maar op dat moment boeten de grote codificaties, zoals de *Code Napoléon*, zelf ook aan belang in. Het meesterlijke evenwicht van de oude Codex wordt dan onmogelijk, een evenwicht waarin de hiërarchische priesterkerk wordt verzoend met het gecodificeerde recht van de rurale samenleving, geconcentreerd rond eigendom en onroerend goed. De *societas perfecta*-leer kon nauwelijks volmaakter concreet gestalte krijgen.

## TWEEDE MOMENTOPNAME: HET KERKELIJK WETBOEK VAN 1983

Toen het kerkelijk wetboek van 1983 tot stand kwam, oogden zowel de kerk als het recht in de profane samenleving fundamenteel anders.

De kerk was doorheen het tweede Vaticaans concilie gegaan, een misschien wat laat maar toch erg reëel *aggiornamento*. De discussies, gebeurtenissen, wendingen, waren soms gewoon spannend. En er kwam heel wat uit de bus: een gevoel van vrijheid, aandacht voor de leek, gevoeligheid voor de rol van de kerk in de wereld, en dat alles zonder spirituele diepgang prijs te geven. Die indruk was toch ontstaan, toen. Hij is in de conciliedocumenten nog steeds terug te vinden, al moet ook worden toegegeven dat wie vandaag deze teksten leest, toch wel voelt dat het om de taal en de stijl van een wat andere tijd gaat. De hoopvolle maar toch al lang vervlogen tijd van de vroege jaren zestig.

De omzetting van het conciliaire gedachtegoed (1962-1965) in een nieuwe Codex (1983) sleepte wat aan. Er gingen achttien jaren overheen. Het was in de canonistiek een periode van ongebreidelde creativiteit, tijdens welke alle mogelijke ideeën konden worden gelanceerd met als enige vereiste: de vertaling van de conciliaire ideeën[4], maar vertaling

---

[4] P. HUIZING, "Hervorming van het kerkelijk recht", *Concilium*, 1965, nr. 8, 96-125; D. FALTIN, "Considerationes quaedam de nova legislationis Ecclesiae ordinatione", *Apollinaris*, 1968, 353-360; G. BALDANZA, "Natura e Fine del Diritto Canonico dopo il Concilio Vaticano II", *Monitor Ecclesiasticus*, 1969, 201-205; P. HUIZING, "Herziening van het kerkelijk wetboek", *Concilium*, 1971, nr. 8, 121-128; P. HUIZING, "De opvatting van het huwelijk in het ontwerp voor een nieuw canoniek huwelijksrecht: kritische aantekeningen", *Bijdragen*, 1977, 72-83.

is niet zelden lieftallig verraad. *Traduttore, traditore,* nietwaar. Dat in deze discussie de idee van een codificatie niet voor iedereen evident was, wekt geen verwondering. Ook in de profane samenleving was de rol van de grote wetboeken nagenoeg uitgespeeld. Dat zelfs de plaats van recht in de kerk ter discussie werd gesteld, gaat al wat verder, en heeft wellicht vaak te maken met een onvermogen recht anders te zien dan op de gesloten, zakelijke, statische wijze waarop het in de Codex van 1917 werd gehanteerd.

Het wetboek dat in 1983 het levenslicht zag, bleef dus wel een wetboek, maar verschilde aanmerkelijk van het vorige. Hoewel het ook nu nog handelde over de hiërarchische inrichting van de kerk, en over de overwegende rol van paus, bisschoppen en priesters geen twijfel liet bestaan, creëerde het toch een aantal openingen voor de leek en voor het vrije initiatief van de gelovigen. De plichten en rechten van alle gelovigen, het statuut van de leek, het verenigingsrecht zijn hiervan sprekende getuigen. Men kan stellen dat het wetboek van 1983 de spanning die in de concilieteksten reeds verscholen lag nog aanscherpte, de spanning tussen enerzijds de overeind blijvende hiërarchische inrichting van de kerk, en anderzijds de ruimte voor bescherming van rechten en vrij initiatief. Het is duidelijk dat hier potentiële conflictstof te signaleren valt[5].

Bij deze 'binnenkerkelijke' tensie zoals het wetboek ze uitdrukt, moet nog een ander spanningsveld worden gevoegd, namelijk de evolutie die het profane recht, onafhankelijk van de ontwikkelingen in de kerk, kende. Het rurale gecodificeerde recht moest stilaan samenleven met de verspreide wetgeving van de sociale welvaartsstaat, met onder meer een uitgebreid sociaal recht, milieurecht, fiscaal recht. En met een alsmaar groeiende aandacht voor de rechten van de persoon, voor mensenrechten ook. Opvallend in dat raam is het toenemende succes van het Europees Verdrag voor de Rechten van de Mens. Het aantal geregistreerde klachten in Straatsburg steeg van 138 in 1955 tot 3.481 in 1995[6]. Natuurlijk is het mogelijk het individualisme dat hiermee gepaard gaat te laken. Waarom al die nadruk op subjectieve rechten, al dat gelijkhebberige

---

[5] M. KUNDERA, *De ondraaglijke lichtheid van het bestaan*, Weesp/Baarn, Agathon/Ambo, 1985, 108: het gaat hier om het ruisen van de semantische rivier, waaronder Kundera begrijpt dat hetzelfde voorwerp telkens weer een andere betekenis opwekt, maar in één adem met die betekenis weerklinkt. Zo heeft het begrip *optocht* een andere betekenis voor iemand die in zijn jeugd, om verstikking tegen te gaan, aan de manifestaties van mei 1968 in Parijs deelneemt dan voor een ander persoon die, als kind, door de Tsjechische overheid wordt verplicht mee op te stappen in obligate stoeten ter ere van het feest van de arbeid.

[6] J. FROWEIN en W. PEUKERT, *Europäische Mensenrechtskonvention: EMRK-Kommentar*, Kehl am Rhein, Engel, 1996, 987.

geprocedeer? En zeker, er zijn excessen. Aan de andere kant rijst de vraag of een overbeklemtonen van mensenrechten – een kenmerk van onze verhalenloze samenleving vandaag – *per se* decadenter of individualistischer is dan het overbeklemtonen van eigendom. Zijn mensenrechten werkelijk moord, terwijl eigendom alleen maar diefstal is? Ook vanuit een christelijk oogpunt lijkt het gemakkelijker zich over de cultus van mensenrechten te buigen dan over de cultus van eigendom. Maar toegegeven, de tegenstelling is niet altijd zo simpel: achter de zogenaamde protectie van mensenrechten schuilt vaak welbegrepen eigenbelang op het materiële vlak.

Hoe dan ook, en hoe ook het morele oordeel moge luiden, er is in het profane recht iets veranderd, namelijk de verschuiving naar de bescherming van rechten toe, een verschijnsel dat op het canonieke vlak niet zonder repercussies kan blijven. Te meer daar dit canoniek recht zelf subjectieve rechten, of iets wat er op lijkt, in zijn systeem heeft opgenomen. Er is dus een dubbel effect. De vernieuwingen in het canoniek recht zelf worden extra in de verf gezet door nieuwe trends in het profane recht.

De indruk bestaat dat het canoniek recht deze vernieuwing nog niet echt heeft geïntegreerd. Terwijl het zopas geschetste probleem naar mijn aanvoelen het centrale thema van de canonistiek in de jaren zeventig en tachtig had moeten zijn, constateert men eerder een terugplooien van het kerkelijk recht op zichzelf. Veel aandacht ging naar de eigen aard van het canoniek recht dat ondanks de schijn, namelijk het bestaan van regels en normen, niet zomaar met het profane recht mocht worden gelijkgesteld[7]. Het heeft een eigen natuur dat uiteraard aan de theologie schatplichtig is. Op een afstand beschouwd zou men kunnen zeggen dat het *societas perfecta*-denken van 1917[8], omstreeks 1983 op een ander échelon werd verdergezet. De verdedigingsgordel werd gewoon verplaatst. Tegenover de alomvattende *societas perfecta* staat voortaan een soort van *ius perfectum*, het volkomen eigen, maar op zichzelf perfect werkbare, recht van de kerk dat een eigen logica heeft

---

[7] L. GEROSA, "*Lex canonica* als *ordinatio fidei*. Einleitende Erwägungen zum Schlüsselbegriff der kanonistischen Lehre von Eugenio Corecco", in L. GEROSA en L. MÜLLER (ed.), *Ordinatio fidei. Schriften zum kanonischen Recht*, Paderborn, F. Schöningh, 1994, IX-XXIII; P. HINDER, *Grundrechte in der Kirche. Eine Untersuchung zur Begründung der Grundrechte in der Kirche*, Freiburg, Universitätsverlag Freiburg, 1977, XIII + 301 p.

[8] F. CAVAGNIS, *Notions de droit public naturel et ecclésiastique*, Parijs-Brussel, Desclée, 1887, 202 e.v.; P. GRANFIELD, "Het verschijnen en verdwijnen van de societas perfecta", *Concilium*, 1982, nr. 7, 8-14; C. TARQUINI, *Iuris ecclesiastici publici institutiones*, Rome, Typis civilitatis catholicae, 1868, VIII + 149 p.

die van de rechtsmechanismen van de profane maatschappij verschilt. Een voorbeeld: de plichten en rechten van alle christengelovigen in de kerk *lijken* voor de oppervlakkige waarnemer wel op de mensenrechten in de profane samenleving, maar verschillen er wezenlijk van om redenen van theologische en ecclesiologische aard[9].

Dit *ius perfectum* komt op het eerste gezicht over als een subtiele reconstructie van de *societas perfecta*. Het heeft bovendien de in onze tijd wat gênante gedachte van een autonome kerk als volmaakte maatschappij niet nodig om toch juridisch zijn eigen gangen te kunnen gaan. De eigenheid zit nu in het recht, niet meer in de maatschappij, maar het effect is hetzelfde.

Of zou hetzelfde moeten zijn. Want anders dan de *societas perfecta* uit 1917, draait het *ius perfectum* uit 1983 soms vierkant.

De eerste reden is dat het wetboek van 1983 dubbelzinniger is dan dat van 1917. De formulering van een aantal canones (bv. can. 208-223 over plichten en rechten, can. 298-329 over het verenigingsrecht) kan minstens de indruk wekken dat zoiets als subjectieve rechten of mensenrechten voortaan in het kerkelijk recht mogelijk zijn. Het vorige wetboek kende die dubbelzinnigheid niet.

De tweede reden waarom het *ius perfectum* van 1983 wankelt, vloeit voort uit de veranderde context van kerk en Codex. Het wetboek richt zich niet alleen tot priesters, die in 1917 beslist insiders waren, maar ook tot leken die allerlei impliciete juridische en theologische kaders minder aanvoelen en aanvaarden.

De derde verklaring voor het wat sputterende *ius perfectum* ligt in de gewijzigde maatschappelijke context. Een gesloten, zakenrechtelijke aanpak strookte in 1917 met de *status quaestionis* in het profane recht. In 1983 neigt dat laatste meer naar een bescherming van rechten, en het is precies hier dat het *ius perfectum* een voet tussen de deur steekt.

Of, anders uitgedrukt, terwijl de symbiose tussen *societas perfecta* en heersend rechtsklimaat in 1917 haast volmaakt tot uitdrukking werd gebracht, vertoont het *ius perfectum* van 1983 spanningsvelden met de codex zelf en met de trends in het profane recht. En wat ook het theologische denken over canoniek recht aanlevert, dat laatste kan teveel tensies met het profane recht niet goed verwerken.

Die spanningen worden in de canonistiek vaak wel onderkend. Ze worden ook door eminente bestuurscanonisten gesignaleerd en beslecht

---

[9] J. HERRANZ CASADO, "Renewal and Effectiveness in Canon Law", *Studia Canonica*, 1994, 5-31.

in het voordeel van wat ik hier het *ius perfectum* heb genoemd[10]. Maar dat is niet altijd genoeg. Soms geven de spanningen aanleiding tot pauselijke uitspraken of wetgeving. Een schoolvoorbeeld is hier de apostolische brief *Ordinatio sacerdotalis* uit 1994[11]. Pogingen om het priesterschap voor vrouwen open te stellen, mogelijk onder meer gebaseerd op het gelijkheidsbeginsel, worden theologisch afgeweerd door er op te wijzen dat de onmogelijkheid vrouwen tot priester te wijden tot de goddelijke ordening van de kerk behoort.

Er is over *Ordinatio sacerdotalis* veel geschreven[12]. Daarbij voeren theologische of zuiver juridische beschouwingen de boventoon. Het is echter ook mogelijk *Ordinatio sacerdotalis* te zien als een bewijs van de onmacht van het *ius perfectum*. Immers, indien de eigen aard van het kerkelijk recht, waarin rechten niet zomaar subjectief zijn en de *communio* geen samenraapsel van individuele belangen[13], algemeen was aanvaard, zou er geen gevaar hebben bestaan voor een bestorming van de wijding via het gelijkheidsbeginsel en de mensenrechten. Om zeker te zijn dat die bestorming niet zou slagen was het nu nodig de goddelijke ordening als grens in te roepen. Een ware receptie van het *ius perfectum* zou zo'n drastische démarche overbodig hebben gemaakt.

Wat voorafgaat, maakt alleszins duidelijk dat de betovering tussen canoniek en profaan recht verbroken is. De harmonie tussen de *societas perfecta*-leer en de profane codificatie werd in de Codex van 1917 meesterlijk gerealiseerd. Het wetboek van 1983 daarentegen staat op gespannen voet met trends in het profane recht. Een eigen *ius perfectum* dat fundamenteel afwijkt van een moderne profane rechtsbenadering werd weliswaar theoretisch mooi uitgebouwd in de rechtsleer, maar wordt niet echt algemeen aanvaard.

---

[10] R.J. CASTILLO LARA, "Some General Reflections on the Rights and Duties of the Christian Faithful", *Studia Canonica*, 1986, 7-32; J. HERRANZ CASADO, "Renewal and Effectiveness in Canon Law", *Studia Canonica*, 1994, 5-31.

[11] IOANNES PAULUS II, Littera apostolica de sacerdotali ordinatione viris tantum reservanda *Ordinatio sacerdotalis*, 22 mei 1994, *AAS*, 1994, 545-548.

[12] D. CITO, "Lettera Apostolica sull'ordinazione sacerdotale da riservarsi soltanto agli uomini, 22 maggio 1994, con nota di D. Cito", *Ius Ecclesiae*, 1995, 347-353; B. FERME, "The Response (28 October 1995) of the Congregation for the Doctrine of the Faith to the Dubium Concerning the Apostolic Letter 'Ordinatio Sacerdotalis' (22 May 1994): Authority and Significance", *Periodica*, 1996, 689-727; W. RABERGER, "Ordinationsfähigkeit der Frau?", *Theologisch-praktische Quartalschrift*, 1996, 398-411; R. TORFS, "Ordinatio sacerdotalis. Kanttekeningen bij een definitief afgesloten discussie", *Onze Alma Mater*, 1994, 282-302.

[13] Cf. canones 210 en 223 § 1 CIC 83.

## DERDE MOMENTOPNAME: HET KERKELIJK RECHT IN 1999

Onopgeloste spanningen die het wetboek van 1983 kenmerken, blijven ook in 1999 nog overeind. Maar tegelijk dient een nieuwe, verrassende ontwikkeling zich aan: de algemeen maatschappelijke belangstelling voor het kerkelijk recht neemt toe. Feiten en gebeurtenissen in de kerk worden door de hedendaagse media vaak via het kerkelijk recht benaderd. Dat is nieuw, ook ten opzichte van 1983. Wellicht kunnen we spreken van een evolutie in drie trappen. In de jaren zestig, tot midden de jaren zeventig werden gebeurtenissen in de kerk vaak becommentarieerd door ecclesiologen en pastoraaltheologen. Daarna, zeg maar omstreeks 1975, maakte de godsdienstsociologische benadering opgeld. En de laatste jaren gaat veel aandacht uit naar een kerkjuridische analyse.

Er is dus een evolutie waar te nemen die vertrekt van een theologische aanpak, en langs een sociologische omweg bij het recht uitkomt. Hoe kan zoiets worden verklaard? Wellicht hierdoor: meer dan andere disciplines is recht vandaag plausibel geworden, een zekere aandacht ervoor en aanvaarding ervan wordt door vele mensen gedeeld. Die plausibiliteit heeft de theologie voor het overgrote deel van de West-Europese bevolking niet meer. De theologische geheimtaal wordt door jongeren, ook intellectuelen, niet meer begrepen. Er bestaat iets als een *emotionele afstand* tussen (jonge) mensen vandaag en theologie en kerk. Niet tegenover het verschijnsel *religie*, dat is wat anders.

Maar hoe dan ook, religie heeft enorm veel met emotie te maken. En precies deze laatste ontbreekt vandaag tegenover de kerk. Emotie is trouwens iets heel vreemds. Ze kan schuilgaan in verloren hoekjes van de kindertijd. Bijvoorbeeld: het lettertype en de lay-out waarin uitnodigingen, affiches, religieuze bladen werden gedrukt in de jaren zestig vermag soms vreemde gevoelens op te roepen: ze waren plots zo anders dan net ervoor. De geur van natte regenjassen in een volle kerk, toen zaterdagavondmissen toegelaten waren, net toegelaten. Jeugdkoren met nieuwe liedjes als afwisseling, als contrast met de bestaande kerkmuziek die daarom alleen nog niet aan het wankelen ging. Dit soort gevoelens, dat vaak te maken heeft met contrasten, en met spanning, omdat ook aandacht spanning is, omdat spanning leven is, kent de hedendaagse mens ten opzichte van de kerk nog nauwelijks. Ze wordt vaak een plaats waar niets gebeurt, behalve bij bijzondere gebeurtenissen. Die worden dan maar best zo objectief mogelijk in kaart gebracht, bij voorkeur door het recht. Theologie biedt alleen de blik van de insider. Sociologie is te abstract en komt soms te intellectualistisch over.

Recht past perfect in het hedendaagse plaatje. Het neemt afstand, maar sluipt via regels toch terug naar concrete feiten toe, zonder dat men zich per se zelf betrokken hoeft te voelen. Daar houden de mensen van, dat herkennen ze. Recht is trouwens ook populair op de televisie.

En er is nog iets anders: recht lijkt niet zo ingewikkeld. Het hangt niet af van doorwrochte intellectualistische constructies. Het heeft meer te maken met gezond boerenverstand. Ook dat is vandaag een pluspunt. Mensen houden niet van intellectualistische constructies, omdat ze zelf geen intellectuelen zijn. Zij bewonderen wel het meer ongrijpbare gezonde boerenverstand, omdat ze de illusie koesteren daar zelf over te beschikken, al ontmoet je zo'n mensen nog minder vaak dan intellectuelen. Maar de schoonheid van de eenvoud is dat ze eenvoudig lijkt.

Kortom, het recht dat niet al te emotioneel is en toch concreet blijft, en dat bovendien niet nodeloos ingewikkeld doet, heeft op het einde van dit millennium behoorlijk wat succes. Het is vaak de sleutel in het wat knarsende slot van geloof en religie. Het is niet zelden een uiting van de schuchtere belangstelling die ook de hedendaagse mens voor religie blijft koesteren, ook al past het niet daar al te openlijk voor uit te komen en ook al ontbreekt een emotionele band met concrete godsdienstbeleving.

Maar hoe dan ook: deze vernieuwde aandacht voor kerkelijk recht blijft niet zonder gevolgen. Ze doet de spanningen die in tekst en toepassing van het wetboek van 1983 al zo zichtbaar waren, nog toenemen. Het kerkelijk recht wordt, omdat het echt recht lijkt ofschoon het zelf beweert dat niet te zijn, plots het visitekaartje van de kerk. Het is niet van de synthese tussen openbarings- en ervaringsgeloof, of van de positie van de geest, dat de hedendaagse mens wakker ligt. Wel van de vraag: zijn de regeltjes eerlijk en worden ze fair toegepast? Dat eerst. Daarna, misschien, het openbarings- en het ervaringsgeloof.

Deze plotse aandacht neemt de kerk wat tegenvoets: het kerkelijk recht is immers al in crisis, presenteert een ambivalent systeem met een *ius perfectum* dat niet boven elke twijfel verheven is. En dan opeens dit: de een beetje boze, wat cynische buitenwereld die de geloofwaardigheid van de kerk aan haar rechtssysteem begint af te meten. Voor de kerk is dit een minder comfortabele positie dan die van 1983, toen men alleen met leken en andere wat moeilijke figuren *binnen* de kerk moest rekening houden. En met 1917, de tijd van een recht voor en door clerici, is elke vergelijking helemaal onmogelijk geworden.

De huidige toestand roept meteen een nieuw spanningsveld in het leven. De vraag die rijst is de volgende: hoe kan aan de geïnteresseerde buitenwereld duidelijk worden gemaakt dat het kerkelijk recht niet zo-maar met het profane recht kan worden gelijkgesteld, doch over een heel eigen natuur beschikt? De opgave is zeker niet gemakkelijk: ook zuiver binnenkerkelijk loopt het met de exacte situering van dat *ius perfectum* niet steeds op wieltjes.


## UITWEGEN

De dialoog *niet* uit de weg gaan lijkt mij nog de beste methode. De profane maatschappij zal immers hoe langer hoe meer impliciete kwali-teitseisen aan het kerkelijk recht stellen, ook via haar rechtspraak op het vlak van kerk en staat. De vraag is dan of een soort *ius perfectum* in ere moet worden gehouden. Ware het ook niet mogelijk om binnen een meer algemeen aanvaard rechtsdenken toch te komen tot de bescherming van wat vanuit een theologisch oogpunt wezenlijk is? In het verleden heb ik reeds vaker in die richting pleidooien gehouden[14], en ik blijf erbij dat zo'n juridisch compromis kan worden gesloten zonder dat er theologisch toegevingen moeten worden gedaan. Beantwoorden aan een moderne rechtscultuur is niet hetzelfde als zwichten voor een mode zonder theo-logische diepgang. En trouwens, het is niet omdat iets geen mode is, dat het wél diepgang heeft.

Maar wil de officiële kerk de dialoog tóch uit de weg gaan, een optie die zeker legaal maar misschien iets minder legitiem is, dan zou ze, voor alle duidelijkheid, zich kunnen uitspreken over het karakter, de eigen aard van haar *ius perfectum*. Zo zou ze bijvoorbeeld het canoniek recht kunnen definiëren als een richtsnoer voor overheidshandelen, waaraan individuen geen concrete rechten kunnen ontlenen, tenzij de overheid ze geval per geval toekent, omdat ze nuttig zijn voor het algemeen welzijn. Het kerkelijk recht zou op die manier ophouden echt recht te zijn, en wordt dan eerder een morele gedragscode voor de overheid[15]. Een terug-val? Ongetwijfeld op het niveau van de intrinsieke juridische kwaliteit.

---

[14] R. TORFS, "Kerkelijk recht in de branding. Terug naar Monseigneur W. Onclin", in R. TORFS (ed.), *Bridging Past and Future. Monsignor W. Onclin Revisited*, Leuven, Peeters, 1998, 19-20.

[15] Ook nu al bevat het kerkelijk wetboek meerdere literaire genres tegelijkertijd, zoals dogmatische verklaringen, theologische meningen, morele verklaringen, geestelijke aan-bevelingen, filosofische theorieën, vaststellingen uit de empirische wetenschappen, voor-schriften die rechten en plichten in het leven roepen. Zie L. ÖRSY, *Theology and Canon Law. New Horizons for Legislation and Interpretation*, Collegeville, The Liturgical Press, 1992, 53-58.

Maar tegelijk is sprake van een vooruitgang op het terrein van rechtsze-kerheid en transparantie. Recht is meer dan canonisten vermoeden ook een vorm van communicatie. En communicatie heeft misschien wat met liefde te maken.

Welke keuze ook wordt gemaakt, uit wat voorafgaat blijkt in ieder geval dat er met recht en reden over een crisis van het kerkelijk recht kan worden gesproken. De spanningen die de Codex van 1983 kenmer-ken, worden door de nieuwe algemeen maatschappelijke belangstelling voor kerkelijk recht nog uitvergroot. Canonisten gaan op deze spannin-gen weinig in. Ze blijven vaak te argeloos uitgaan van de plausibiliteit van een autonoom kerkelijk recht dat wezenlijk harmonisch blijft. Ten tijde van de oude Codex kon dit nog. Maar vandaag op exact dezelfde wijze canonieke problemen aanpakken als twintig, dertig jaar geleden, is een kwalitatieve achteruitgang. Wat eertijds een correcte benadering was, is nu een kortzichtige aanpak. De jaren verkleuren het gelijk.

Aan de ander kant biedt de crisis nieuwe kansen. Dat het canoniek recht niet alleen priesters, maar ook leken en zelfs neutrale burgers van een geseculariseerde samenleving aanspreekt, creëert een pak moeilijk-heden, maar biedt ook onverwachte mogelijkheden. Zo kan het canoniek recht, als het kundig wordt uitgewerkt en authentiek is, een brugfunctie vervullen tussen de lichtjes decadente maar niet altijd ongezellige pro-fane samenleving enerzijds, en de diepzinnige maar wat ontoegankelijke theologische en kerkelijke wereld anderzijds. Precies omdat die taak zo belangrijk oogt, is de kans op een mislukking zeer reëel. Maar een mis-lukking met een dergelijke allure, en dat in een debat waarbij zoveel op het spel staat, was in het raam van het oude wetboek gewoon onmoge-lijk geweest. Dat laatste was immers het verfijnde behangselpapier van een netjes gesloten burgerlijke huiskamer. Kortom, er is nu wat verwar-ring. Maar er is ook vooruitgang. De winst ligt in de kans op écht grote mislukkingen. Zoveel eer oogstte het canoniek recht de laatste eeuwen zelden.

# CRISIS IN CANON LAW

R. Torfs

## WHAT CRISIS?

Can one speak of a crisis in canon law? Certainly not if one looks at the number of academic institutions offering courses in canon law, since the list is constantly growing: Budapest, Mexico City, Rome, Yaoundé[1]. Moreover, legislators in canon law are quite active and the media exhibit a lively interest in the law of the church. Yet the situation is not as healthy as it may seem. Canon law's place as a discipline is becoming less and less clear, and the debate about its place is more subdued compared with a few decades ago[2]. And even though there are now more courses than ever, there are fewer great practitioners of canon law, fewer people who can be considered a landmark in their discipline, people who may be either supported or rejected but who, in any case, are clearly present. Great canonists pass away[3], but they are not born: they emerge only very slowly after years of growth and development. And yet, despite these attempts at consolation, there remains a certain scarcity. In the face of more courses, more legislation and more media attention, there are fewer intellectual debates and fewer noteworthy canonists. Does this point to a crisis? I am afraid it points, at the very least, to something of a decline. How has it come to this? I would like to offer my personal view of the situation, one which is subjective, or at least not objective in the classical sense, not distanced and unprejudiced. This subjective approach means that I write from the point of view of Western Europe, since I have simply no other choice, and that I decline to use a culturally pessimistic explanatory model, characterized by attacks on the modern person's narcissism, individualism and egoism, for I am one myself, especially as far as the negative aspects are concerned.

---

[1] Budapest, 30 November 1996; Mexico-City, 4 September 1995; Rome, Ateneo Romano della Santa Croce, 28 March 1993; Yaoundé, 15 November 1991.

[2] S. BERLINGÒ, *L'ultimo diritto. Tensioni escatologiche nell'ordine dei sistemi*, Torino, G. Giappichelli, 1998, 258 p.

[3] E. Corecco (1931 - 1995), P. Gismondi (†1986), P.A. d'Avack (†1982), P. Lombardía (1930 - 1986), W. Onclin (1905 - 1989), P. Huizing (1911 - 1995).

The crisis of canon law – or the decline – can perhaps be explained on the basis of three snapshots: the 1917 code of canon law, the 1983 code and finally a bill of health from 1999, where we are teetering on the edge of yet another millenium.

## FIRST SNAPSHOT: THE 1917 CODE OF CANON LAW

The 1917 code of canon law, brainchild of Pietro Gasparri, was a product of the war. It came about during World War I, at a significant historical fault line, when Europe seemed to be voluntarily squandering its own hegemony. The democratization of society was waiting in the wings. There was a strange hesitation in the air between a despondent leniency and an innovative daring. It was the atmosphere of Thomas Mann's *Magic Mountain*. The perfect moment, then, for a legal code, and Gasparri rose to the occasion. He delivered a harmonious piece of work. The code reflected the church at that time, a hierarchical church of priests in which the position of lay people, for instance, was hardly a matter of discussion. And there was not much call for such discussion in any case. Of the code's five books, *De rebus* was particularly noteworthy. The book *De rebus* comprised 826 of the 2414 canons. Indeed, the law of sacraments in its entirety was considered a part of the law of (material) 'things', of goods. For theologians and commentators in the Sixties, this was a curse. How could the sacraments, with all their theological richness, be reduced to the law of things, that sober discipline of civil law engaged in the description of property and usufruct, buildings and hereditary tenure? Though such indignation is best treated with caution, the old categorization is not completely illogical. In the first place, in 1917, just as in all the major 19th-century codifications, the law of things, with its focus on the continuing value of immovable goods, was the keystone of rural society and the most significant branch of law. That which was valuable enjoyed protection in the law of things, so the sacraments were in good company there. In addition, placing the sacraments under the law of things provides the greatest possible degree of clarity: static clarity, admittedly, but clarity nonetheless. The sacraments stand as a house, literally. The soft certainty of immovable goods.

In fact, the 1917 codex is a consistent working out of the theory of the *societas perfecta*. For those who adhere to the church, it is a total society, like any other. It is not merely contained within society; it is a society itself, with its own laws which treat sacraments as real things, just as real as the houses that populate profane society in the 19th and early 20th centuries. It is only when property becomes theft that a sacrament is no longer a thing. But at that moment, the great codifications, such as the Napoleonic Code, also lose their importance. The careful balance achieved by the old codex is then no longer possible, a balance where the hierarchical priestly church was reconciled with the codified law of rural society, emphasizing property and immovable goods. The theory of the *societas perfecta* could hardly have had a more perfect expression.

## SECOND SNAPSHOT: THE 1983 CODE OF CANON LAW

When the 1983 code of canon law was produced, both the church and the law in profane society had fundamentally changed. The church had undergone the second Vatican council, a perhaps belated but still very real *aggiornamento*. The discussions, events and paths followed were sometimes charged with tension, and a great deal happened as a result: a sense of freedom, attention to the laity, sensitivity to the church's role in the world – all without having to compromise spiritual depth. This was the impression that arose at the time. It can still be read in the conciliar documents, though it must be admitted that anyone reading those texts today also gets a feeling that they are in the language and style of a different era: the hopeful and yet remote time of the early Sixties.

Converting these conciliar ideas (1962-1965) into a new codex (1983) dragged out over eighteen years. It was a period of unbridled creativity in canon law, when all possible ideas could be floated, the only requirement being that they translate conciliar ideas[4]. Translation, however, is not infrequently a charming betrayal: *traduttore, traditore*. It comes as no surprise that, in this discussion, the idea of codification was not obvious to everyone. In profane society as well, the role of the great codex had pretty much been played out. But the fact that the very role of law as such in the church came under discussion was already a significant

---

[4] P. HUIZING, "The Reform of Canon Law", *Concilium*, 1965, n° 8, 95-128; D. FALTIN, "Considerationes quaedam de nova legislationis Ecclesiae ordinatione", *Apollinaris*, 1968, 353-360; G. BALDANZA, "Natura e Fine del Diritto Canonico dopo il Concilio Vaticano II", *Monitor Ecclesiasticus*, 1969, 201-205; P. HUIZING, "The Revision of Canon Law", *Concilium*, 1971, n° 8, 124-134; P. HUIZING, "De opvatting van het huwelijk in het ontwerp voor een nieuw canoniek huwelijksrecht: kritische aantekeningen", *Bijdragen*, 1977, 72-83.

step, probably having to do with an inability to view the law otherwise than in the closed, businesslike and static way in which the 1917 codex had treated it.

The codex which first saw the light of day in 1983 was still a book of law, but it differed markedly from the previous one. While it still discussed matters such as the hierarchical structure of the church, and gave no cause for doubt about the paramount role of the Pope, bishops and priests, it nevertheless created a number of openings for lay people and for the exercise of free initiative on the part of believers. The duties and rights of every believer, the status of the laity and the right to association all bear eloquent witness to this. One could say that the 1983 codex even sharpened the already existing tension that was latent in the conciliar texts: the tension between the remaining hierarchical structure in the church, on the one hand, and the space created for the protection of rights and free initiative on the other. It is clear that potential material for conflict can be found here[5].

This tension internal to the church, as expressed in the codex, must be supplemented by another field of tension, namely the evolution of profane law, independent of developments in the church. The codified law of a rural society gradually had to make room for the expanding legislation of the social welfare state with, among other things, extensive social law, environmental law, tax law, as well as growing attention to the rights of the person and human rights in general. Noteworthy in this regard is the increasing success enjoyed by the European Convention on Human Rights: the number of complaints registered in Strasbourg increased from 138 in 1955 to 3.481 in 1995[6]. Of course it is possible to condemn the unbridled individualism that came with this. Why all the emphasis on subjective rights, all the righteously argumentative litigation? And admittedly, there have been excesses. On the other hand, one could raise the question whether an over-emphasis on human rights – characteristic of contemporary society's lack of narratives – is any more decadent or individualistic *per se* than the over-emphasis on property. Are human rights really murder, whereas property is only theft? From a Christian point of

---

[5] M. KUNDERA, *The Unbearable Lightness of Being*, London/Boston, Faber and Faber, 1985, 99: Kundera is talking about the flowing of the semantic river. The same word has for different people a different meaning. The word 'parade' has another meaning for someone who participates in the manifestations of May 1968 in Paris than for another person who was, as a child, forced by the Czech authorities to participate in the obligatory May Day parades.

[6] J. FROWEIN and W. PEUKERT, *Europäische Mensenrechtskonvention: EMRK-Kommentar*, Kehl am Rhein, Engel, 1996, 987.

view as well, it seems easier to accept the cult of human rights than the cult of property. Granted though, the opposition is not always so simple: lurking behind the so-called protection of human rights is often an unambiguous material self-interest.

In spite of all this, and whatever the moral judgement may be, something has changed in profane law: the shift towards the protection of rights, a phenomenon that cannot fail to have repercussions in the area of canon law. All the more so because canon law has itself assumed subjective rights, or something that closely resembles them, into its system. There is then a double effect. New tendencies in canon law are given an even greater emphasis by new trends in profane law.

One gets the impression that canon law has not yet really integrated these new tendencies. While the problem just mentioned should, in my opinion, have been the central theme of canon law in the Seventies and Eighties, what one actually sees is canon law turning in upon itself. A great deal of attention was given to the specific nature of canon law which, despite appearances – i.e., the existence of rules and norms – could not simply be equated with profane law[7]. It has its own nature, one that is clearly indebted to theology. Viewed from a distance, one could say that the *societas perfecta* idea from 1917[8] was pursued on another level around 1983. The line of defence was simply shifted. As opposed to the comprehensive *societas perfecta* there is henceforth a sort of *ius perfectum*, a completely unique but nevertheless perfectly workable law of the church, with its own logic which is different from the legal mechanisms of profane society. For example, to a superficial observer, the duties and rights of all Christian believers in the church look similar to the human rights of profane society, but they are essentially different for reasons of a theological and ecclesiastical nature[9].

This *ius perfectum* looks at first sight to be a subtle reconstruction of the *societas perfecta*. Moreover, it has no need of the nowadays somewhat embarrassing notion of the autonomous church as a perfect society

[7] L. GEROSA, "*Lex canonica* als *ordinatio fidei*. Einleitende Erwägungen zum Schlüsselbegriff der kanonistischen Lehre von Eugenio Corecco", in L. GEROSA and L. MÜLLER (ed.), *Ordinatio fidei. Schriften zum kanonischen Recht*, Paderborn, F. Schöningh, 1994, IX-XXIII; P. HINDER, *Grundrechte in der Kirche. Eine Untersuchung zur Begründung der Grundrechte in der Kirche*, Freiburg, Universitätsverlag Freiburg, 1977, XIII + 301 p.

[8] F. CAVAGNIS, *Notions de droit public naturel et ecclésiastique*, Paris-Brussels, Desclée, 1887, 202 e.v.; P. GRANFIELD, "The Rise and Fall of *Societas Perfecta*", *Concilium*, 1982, n° 7, 3-9; C. TARQUINI, *Iuris ecclesiastici publici institutiones*, Rome, Typis civilitatis catholicae, 1868, VIII + 149 p.

[9] J. HERRANZ CASADO, "Renewal and Effectiveness in Canon Law", *Studia Canonica*, 1994, 5-31.

in order to follow its own legal path. Its specificity now resides in the law, and no longer in society, but the effect is the same.

Or at least it should have been the same, for in contrast to the *societas perfecta* of 1917, the *ius perfectum* of 1983 sometimes misses the mark. The first reason for this is that the 1983 codex is more ambiguous than the one from 1917. The formulation of a number of the canons (e.g., 208-223 concerning duties and rights, 298-329 concerning the right to association) might give rise to the impression that something like subjective rights or human rights are henceforth a possibility in canon law. The previous codex did not contain this ambiguity. The second reason why the *ius perfectum* of 1983 falters is a result of the changed context of the church and the codex. The codex is not only directed to priests, who were definitely insiders in 1917, but also to lay people who are less sensitive to, and less willing to accept many implicit legal and theological frameworks. The third explanation for the somewhat spasmodic success of *ius perfectum* lies in the altered social context. A closed approach, stressing the law of things, was in keeping with the *status quaestionis* in profane law in 1917. In 1983, profane law tends more towards the protection of rights, and this is precisely where *ius perfectum* gets its foot in the door. In other words, while the symbiosis between *societas perfecta* and the dominant legal climate was almost perfectly expressed in 1917, the *ius perfectum* of 1983 exhibits tensions with the codex itself and with the trends in profane law. And whatever theological thought might be able to say about canon law, canon law cannot easily endure too many tensions with profane law.

These tensions are often underestimated. They are also pointed out and resolved by eminent canonists in favour of what I have here called *ius perfectum*[10]. But that is not always enough. The tensions are sometimes the occasion for papal pronouncements or legislation. A clear example of this is the 1994 apostolic letter, *Ordinatio sacerdotalis*[11]. Attempts to open the priesthood to women, possibly on the basis of the principle of equality, were theologically refuted by indicating that the impossibility of ordaining women is part of the divine order of the church.

---

[10] R.J. CASTILLO LARA, "Some General Reflections on the Rights and Duties of the Christian Faithful", *Studia Canonica*, 1986, 7-32; J. HERRANZ CASADO, "Renewal and Effectiveness in Canon Law", *Studia Canonica*, 1994, 5-31.

[11] IOANNES PAULUS II, Littera apostolica de sacerdotali ordinatione viris tantum reservanda *Ordinatio sacredotalis*, 22 May 1994, *AAS*, 1994, 545-548.

Much has been written about *Ordinatio sacerdotalis*[12], and most of the considerations are of a theological or strictly legal nature. It is, however, perfectly possible to view *Ordinatio sacerdotalis* as proof of the impotence of *ius perfectum*, for if there were a general acceptance of the specific nature of canon law, whereby rights are not simply subjective and the *communio* is not simply a collection of individual interests[13], then there would have been no danger of an attack on ordination by way of the principle of equality and human rights. In order to ensure that this attack did not succeed, it was necessary to invoke divine order as a limitation. A true reception of *ius perfectum* would have made such a drastic response superfluous.

All of this goes to show that the allure between canon law and profane law has been broken. The harmony between the theory of the *societas perfecta* and profane codification was masterfully embodied in the 1917 codex. The 1983 codex, on the contrary, is out of step with developments in profane law. It is true that a specific *ius perfectum*, fundamentally different from a modern, profane approach to the law, has been consistently worked out in legal theory, but it has not really been generally accepted.

## THIRD SNAPSHOT: CANON LAW IN 1999

The unresolved tensions characteristic of the 1983 codex are still in force in 1999. At the same time however, there is a surprising new development: the general social interest in canon law is on the increase. The media often interpret facts and events in the church by way of canon law. This is something new, even compared with 1983. We might speak of a three stage evolution. From the Sixties to the mid-Seventies, events in the church were often commented upon by experts in ecclesiology and pastoral theologians. After that, around 1975, there was an increasing reliance on the approach of religious sociology. And in recent years, a great deal of attention is being paid to analyses in canon law.

---

[12] D. CITO, "Lettera Apostolica sull'ordinazione sacerdotale da riservarsi soltanto agli uomini, 22 maggio 1994, con nota di D. Cito", *Ius Ecclesiae*, 1995, 347-353; B. FERME, "The Response (28 October 1995) of the Congregation for the Doctrine of the Faith to the Dubium Concerning the Apostolic Letter *Ordinatio Sacerdotalis* (22 May 1994): Authority and Significance", *Periodica*, 1996, 689-727; W. RABERGER, "Ordinationsfähigkeit der Frau?", *Theologisch-praktische Quartalschrift*, 1996, 398-411; R. TORFS, "Ordinatio sacerdotalis. Kanttekeningen bij een definitief afgesloten discussie", *Onze Alma Mater*, 1994, 282-302.
[13] Cf. canons 210 and 223 § 1, CIC 83.

One can see an evolution, then, moving from a theological approach, passing by way of sociology, towards the law. How can this be explained? Perhaps in the following way: more than most other disciplines today, the law has become plausible, with a certain interest in the law and acceptance of it being shared by many people. For the vast majority of the Western European population, theology no longer has this plausibility. The secret language of theology is no longer understood by young people, even intellectuals. There exists today something like an *emotional gap* separating (young) people from theology or the church, though not from the phenomenon of religion as such. There the situation is somewhat different.

In any case, religion has a great deal to do with emotion, and this is precisely what is lacking nowadays in regard to the church. Emotion is something quite strange. It can be found lurking in the hidden corners of our youth. For instance: the layout and font used in the Sixties for printing invitations, posters, and religious announcements was sometimes capable of evoking strange emotions. They were suddenly so different from what went before. The smell of wet raincoats in a full church when Saturday evening mass was still new, or youth choirs with new songs in contrast to the existing church music which was not yet under threat. These sorts of feelings, have to do with contrasts, with tensions (because attention is also a kind of tension, because tension is life) and therefore they are no longer part of a contemporary person's experience of the church. In many cases, the church has become a place where nothing happens, except in exceptional cases, and then they are handled as objectively as possible, preferably by the law. Theology only offers an insider's view. Sociology is too abstract and sometimes comes across as too intellectual.

The law fits in perfectly with the contemporary picture. It takes a distance, but also slips back into concrete fact by way of rules, without the need to involve anyone personally. People like this; they recognize it. The law is also popular on television.

And there is a further reason: the law does not seem overly complicated. It does not depend on well thought-out intellectual constructions, but has more to do with good old-fashioned common sense. That is an advantage nowadays. People do not like intellectual constructions since they are not intellectuals themselves. They admire the more ineffable old-fashioned common sense because they harbour the illusion that they are in possession of it, although one encounters such people less often than intellectuals even. Yet the beauty of simplicity is precisely that it seems so simple.

In short, it is the law – being not too emotional and yet still concrete, and also not unnecessarily complicated – that enjoys a good degree of success at the end of this millennium. It is often the key in the rather creaky lock of faith and religion. Not infrequently, it is an expression of the tentative interest that contemporary people still exhibit for religion, even though it would be inappropriate to show this too openly, and even though there is a lack of emotional links with a concrete experience of religion.

Whatever may be the case, this renewed interest in canon law is not without consequences. It intensifies the tensions that were already so apparent in the text and application of the 1983 codex. Canon law has suddenly become the church's calling card, because it looks like real law, though it claims that it is not. No one these days is concerned about the synthesis of revelation and experience in belief, or about the place of the spirit, but they are concerned about the question whether the rules are honest and whether they are applied fairly. That comes first, and only secondarily, if at all, the question of revelation and experience in belief.

This sudden attention has taken the church a bit by surprise. Canon law was already in crisis, presenting an ambivalent system with a *ius perfectum* that is not above all doubt, and then suddenly this: the angry, rather cynical outside world begins to judge the church's credibility by its legal system. For the church, this is a less comfortable position than in 1983, when it only had to take account of lay people and other difficult figures *within* the church. And certainly any comparison with 1917, when there was a law by and for clerics, has become utterly impossible.

The current situation immediately generates a new field of tension. The question that arises is the following: how can one make clear to the interested outside world that canon law cannot simply be equated with profane law, but that it has its own unique nature? This is certainly not an easy task. Even within the church, an exact situating of *ius perfectum* is not always so simple.

## SOLUTIONS

It seems to me that dialogue is still the best method. More and more, profane society will place quality demands on canon law, by way of jurisprudence in the area of church and state. The question then is whether something like *ius perfectum* should be retained. Might it be possible, within a more generally accepted legal theory, to arrive at some protection for what is essential from a theological point of view? In the past, I have often put forward arguments in this direction[14], and I remain convinced that this kind of legal compromise can be found without having to make theological concessions. Being answerable to a modern legal culture is not the same as yielding to a fashion without any theological depth. On the other hand, the fact that something is not a fashion does not mean that it has depth.

Yet if the official church still wants to avoid dialogue – a perfectly legal, though perhaps less legitimate choice – then in the interest of clarity it could make a statement about the character and the specific nature of its *ius perfectum*. For example, it could define canon law as a guideline for governmental action, from which individuals cannot derive any concrete rights, unless the government grants them on a case by case basis because they are useful for the general welfare. In this way, canon law would really cease to be law, instead becoming more of a moral code of conduct for the government[15]. Is that a setback? Undoubtedly it would be at the level of intrinsic legal quality. But at the same time it would constitute progress in the area of legal security and transparency. The law is also a form of communication, more than canonists might suspect. And communication perhaps has something to do with love.

Whatever the choice made, from what we have seen it is clear that one can legitimately speak of a crisis in canon law. The tensions characteristic of the 1983 codex are intensified by the new general social interest in canon law. But canonists rarely examine these tensions. Most often, they still innocently believe in the plausibility of an autonomous canon law which is essentially harmonious. This was still possible at the time of the old codex, but to deal with problems in canon law today in the same way as twenty or thirty years ago represents a decline in quality. What was at that time a correct approach is nowadays short-sighted. The years affect what is considered right.

On the other hand, the crisis creates new opportunities. The fact that canon law has something to offer, not only to priests but also to lay

[14] R. TORFS, "Canon Law in the Balance. Monsignor W. Onclin Revisited", in R. TORFS (ed.), *Bridging Past and Future. Monsignor W. Onclin Revisited*, Leuven, Peeters, 1998, 29-30.

[15] Even now we can find in the Code of Canon Law several literary forms concurrently, such as dogmatic statements, theological opinions, statements of morality, spiritual exhortations, theories borrowed from philosophers, affirmations borrowed from empirical statements, canons creating right and duty situations. See L. ÖRSY, *Theology and Canon Law. New Horizons for Legislation and Interpretation*, Collegeville, The Liturgical Press, 1992, 53-58.

people and even neutral citizens of a secularized society, creates a host of difficulties but also provides unexpected possibilities. Canon law, if carefully worked out and authentic, can build a bridge between the slightly decadent but not always unpleasant profane society on the one hand, and the profound but somewhat inaccessible theological and religious world on the other. Precisely because this task seems so important, the chance of failure is very real. But a failure with such allures, in a debate where so much is at stake, would have been impossible in the context of the old codex, which was something like the elegant wallpaper in an enclosed bourgeois sitting room. In short, there is some confusion now. But there is also progress. The benefits lie in the possibility of a really large failure. Canon law has seldom gained so much to its credit in recent centuries.

# WAYS AND MEANS OF THE INTERNATIONAL ACTIVITY OF THE HOLY SEE

C. MIGLIORE

## I. DIPLOMACY AND THE HOLY SEE

More than 50 years ago, Stalin, exasperated over the continuous references to the Pope of Rome, asked: "How many army divisions does the Pope have?" In other words, why speak about the Pope if he doesn't have any real power. Obviously, Stalin did not know that 40 years later the very regime that he was sustaining would fall also as a result of these invisible, but effective, divisions.

We speak today about the diplomacy of the Holy See. Diplomacy and Holy See – that seems to be a contradiction in terms. In fact, diplomacy is a word full of meaning. There are those who define it as the art of negotiating; others as the technique of regulating relations between States; and still others as the application of the principles of diplomatic law. The popular notion is often Machiavelli's: "Diplomacy is the art of getting what you want at any cost and by any means." How can the Holy See accept this concept of diplomacy?

The Holy See participates in diplomacy in order to have its voice heard within the international community. However, it does not rest its diplomacy upon the strength of military power or economic strength. Rather, the diplomacy of the Holy See has characteristics which are different from those of the countries of the world.

In short, these questions arise: Why is the Holy See present and active on the international scene? Why does the Holy See exercise diplomacy to the degree that countries do? Why does she exercise diplomacy which is the prerogative of sovereign Nations?

The response to these questions will emerge, I hope, in the course of this reflection.

The first point to examine then is the nature of the Holy See.

## II. HOLY SEE OR THE VATICAN?

The "Holy See" is the Pope, together with all the bodies of the Roman Curia through which he governs the Catholic Church. The Holy See is a sovereign juridical person because it is the supreme organ of the Catholic Church. Its existence as a sovereign subject is recognised in international law. It is the Holy See, and not Vatican City that is the juridical interlocutor within the international community.

In 1929, the Vatican State was created by the agreement between the Holy See and the Kingdom of Italy. They decided to establish Vatican City in order to assure the Pope a basis for his absolute independence and autonomy from any earthly power. The Treaty of 1929 specifies that "the Holy See is sovereign to Vatican City."

The Vatican is intended only to ensure independence for the action of the Holy See, thanks to a territorial sovereignty reduced to its minimum expression. The Vatican does not pursue the aims that are proper to a country, which has to guarantee the political, social and economic rights of its population, etc.

When the newspapers speak about the establishment of diplomatic relations between the Holy See and a country, they usually say: "The Vatican" is sending an Ambassador, for instance, to Israel or Russia. However, it is not the little Vatican City State that is the subject of international law acting in bilateral or multilateral relations in Washington, New York, Geneva or Kinshasa. It is always the Holy See that is acting.

## III. WHY IS THE HOLY SEE A SOVEREIGN SUBJECT OF INTERNATIONAL LAW?

Why is the Holy See sovereign in international law, in the same way as a State?

There are two reasons: one comes from history, and the other from the concept the Church has of herself.

A) The Historical Perspective

The primacy of the Bishop of Rome was clearly asserted in the early centuries of the Church's existence and was evident when the Pope despatched special envoys, entrusting them with the mission of carrying messages of peace and of evaluating local Churches. Towards the 6th and 7th centuries, like the Emperor in the East, the Bishop of Rome recognised the usefulness of keeping a representative at the Court of Constantinople, in order to convey his requests and advice and to receive the replies. Later on, when the christological disputes and wrangling over images had estranged Byzantium and Rome, relations were established between the Frankish Court and the See of Rome. It was, thanks to the Carolingian Kings, Pepin the Short and Charlemagne, that the Bishop of Rome became ruler of the Eternal City and other territory. The foundation and the subsequent consolidation of the Papal States lead to a series of ambassadorial missions between the Frankish Court and the Roman Pontiff.

During the 15th and 16th centuries the prestige of the papacy was shaken, on the one hand, by the Great Western Schism and on the other, by the nations who asserted their autonomy by repudiating the authority of papal legates with extensive powers. In order to safeguard her essential rights, the Church considered it appropriate not to insist too much on plenipotentiary legates, because it was precisely the power of the Church that was being contested. Rather she made efforts to protect her rights through persuasion and reconciliation undertaking long years of delicate negotiations.

Finally, the 15th century favoured the consolidation of the States on the peninsula: Venice, Florence, Naples, Milan and Rome, where the authority of the Pope had so often been checked by the body politic and the feudality of Latium. Princes and cities confronted one another violently, but, just as much as the force of arms, diplomacy constituted a real factor in victory. It is in this geographical and historical context that historians place the birth of modern diplomacy and permanent embassies. It is also the period in which the evolution of the Papal Representations begins: temporary Legations become permanent Nunciatures. In passing from the rank of a legation to that of a nunciature, pontifical representation was taking part in the general evolution which led States to establish embassies.

The Council of Trent, peace between the christian princes, as well as the defence and the alliance against the Turks were the first major questions entrusted to the competence and zeal of the Pontifical Representatives. In

Spain, France, Portugal, Poland and certain provinces of the Habsburgs, Princes possessed the right of appointing Bishops and Abbots by pontifical concession or custom. Nomination by the King of France, presentation by the King of Spain, recommendation by the King of Poland, whatever the formula used the subject was designated by the Prince and confirmed by the Pope, in accordance with canon law, but only after a local enquiry had been conducted to verify the dignity of the candidate. It was the task of the Nuncios to prepare the dossier and to gather the information by questioning witnesses. If the information proved unfavourable, it was for the Nuncio to convince the Sovereign to renounce his candidate and select another. It is evident that only a Representative of the Pope, who was residing in the place, could be in a position to gather in depth information, anticipate undesirable candidacies and negotiate the necessary withdrawal of an unfortunate nomination with a sovereign jealous of his prerogatives.

The discussion at the Congress of Vienna of 1815 is rightly well known. On the controversial question of the precedence of ambassadors on the basis of the date of presentation of Letters of Credence, the Congress recognises the Nuncio as having the rank of Dean, with the historic phrase – "the present rule does not involve any change regarding the Representative of the Pope", thus officially sanctioning the privilege enjoyed by the Representatives of the Holy See at the Catholic Courts. This recognition was confirmed at the Conference of the United Nations in 1961.

During the fifty nine years when papal authority was stripped of all territorial foundation – a result of the capture of Rome in 1870, to be re-established by the Lateran Treaty in 1929 – the Holy See did not reduce its diplomatic activity in any way: the Legates of the Roman Pontiff were despatched throughout the world; the numbers of States officially represented before the Pope doubled, going from fourteen to thirty; fifty or more bilateral documents were signed; a dozen or so cases calling for arbitration and international mediation were deferred to the Pontiff. Moreover, it were non-catholic sovereigns like Kaiser William II, Tzar Nicholas II and Queen Wilhelmina who took the initiative to ensure that the Holy See's advice would be admitted to the international conclaves at the time of the Conferences of Berlin and the Hague at the end of the 19th century.

Since the disappearance of the Papal States, the number of Nunciatures has never ceased to grow: as we have seen, of the fourteen nunciatures then in existence the number reached thirty at the beginning of this century, then sixty in the period after the Second World War. Numerous peoples who formerly depended politically on the great Empires now gained their sovereignty, such as the countries of Latin America in the 19th century and the African States in the 20th century. In addition, some Asian and Near Eastern countries now have relations with the Holy See. Some twenty countries who call themselves "muslim" have also wished to establish diplomatic relations with the Holy See. When Pope John Paul II was elected to the See of Peter, on 16 October 1978, ninety states were represented before the Holy See. The number continues to increase. At the present moment there are 169; of those some 23 nunciatures have been created or reopened in Eastern European countries, notably in the republics which have replaced the Soviet Union since its collapse, as well as the former Yugoslavia.

In 1948, FAO was the first international organisation to receive a permanent Observer from the Holy See. This was to be followed by the World Health Organisation and the International Labour Organisation in Geneva. In 1951, the Apostolic See entered the UN system, becoming a member of the executive Council of the High Commissioner for Refugees. In 1952, Monsignor Roncalli, who was to become Pope John XXIII, joined to his mission of Apostolic Nuncio in Paris the task of being the first pontifical Observer to UNESCO. In 1956, the Holy See symbolically ratified the creation of the International Atomic Energy Authority and since 1966 it has named an observer to the United Nations Industrial Development Organisation in Vienna. As regards other European institutions, the Holy See became a member of the Council for Cultural Co-operation of the Council of Europe in 1962, and since 1974 a Special Envoy with the functions of a Permanent Observer is residing in Strasbourg. An Apostolic Nuncio is also accredited to the European Union. In 1972, the Holy See was a "participant" in the diplomatic Conference which we know today by the abbreviation OSCE (Organisation for Security and Co-operation in Europe). Finally, the Nuncio in Washington is also the Permanent Observer to the Organisation of American States.

B) The Nature of the Church

The Church has always held that she is independent of any political power. Historically, this is something peculiar to the Catholic Church. The Orthodox Churches, heirs of Byzantium, have all become State

Churches, identified with a particular nation; and each national Church has wanted to be autocephalous, independent of the other Churches, but subject to the political power of its own Country. Most Protestant Churches, and especially Anglican and Lutheran Churches, have done the same. The temporal ruler has become the supreme Head of the national Church. The Catholic Church, for her part, has always maintained that she is a supranational community and does not receive her legal existence from any temporal State. The Catholic Church exists as such, and it is in the Holy See that her organic unity is guaranteed, represented and perpetuated. Her extension corresponds to the dissemination of Catholic believers throughout the world. She is therefore a universal community, that knows no national frontiers. The juridical form in which the Church enters into a relationship with sovereign States is, therefore, the Holy See, which is the personification – the technical term – of the autonomy, independence and sovereignty proper to the Catholic Church. It is the Holy See, and not the Vatican State, that is the juridical interlocutor, both for the States and for the international community.

To clarify these ideas, we must always recall, as stated above, that between 1870 and 1929 the Pope had no State. And yet, the Holy See continued to act on the international scene: accrediting Nuncios, signing Concordats and acting as an international arbiter, even at the request of Bismarck, who was a protestant. The Holy See did not even suffer at the level of its international juridical personality when she lost her States, because it is not by virtue of any territorial sovereignty that the Holy See is sovereign on the international level.

## IV. BILATERAL DIPLOMATIC ACTIVITY OF THE HOLY SEE

Today the diplomacy of the Holy See is not only recognised in international law and within the order of international affairs, but its presence is sought after and its activity is appreciated. In fact, a diplomatic representative of the Holy See is accredited to almost all the countries of the world, and the new countries which have appeared as a result of the end of colonialism decades ago and the dissolution of the socialist bloc a few years ago were eager to establish diplomatic relations with the Holy See at the level of Nunciature.

Currently, the Holy See has diplomatic relations with 169 countries and is accredited with an Apostolic Nuncio for the European Union, a

Representative at OSCE and Permanent Observers at the United Nations in New York, Geneva and Vienna, as well as at UNESCO in Paris, FAO in Rome, the Organisation of American States in Washington and the Council of Europe in Strasbourg.

Obviously, the Holy See does not maintain a Nunciature and a Nuncio in each of the countries with which it has diplomatic relations. Rather, 101 Nunciatures cover the 169 countries and 6 permanent missions follow the international organisations.

Among the countries that do not yet have relations with the Holy See we find:
- in Africa: Mauritania, West Sahara, Somalia and Gibuti;
- in Asia: China, Vietnam, Laos, North Korea, Afghanistan, Malaysia and Myanmar;
- in the Middle East: Saudi Arabia, Oman, Bahrain, Qatar and the United Arab Emirates.

It is interesting to note, that, with the exception of Saudi Arabia and some of the countries of the Arab Peninsula, almost all the so-called "islamic" countries, that is, those with a predominant islamic population, have established diplomatic relations with the Holy See during the second half of this century.

The personnel of the Holy See's diplomatic service who have diplomatic rank is rather limited considering the amount of work that exists: 107 Heads of Mission (Nuncios and Permanent Observers) and about 150 lower level personnel.

The same is true in the Section for Relations with States of the Secretary of State in the Vatican, which corresponds to a Ministry of Foreign Affairs. It is headed by a Secretary (equivalent to a Minister) and an Under-Secretary. It is composed of about 40 desk-officers who have rather large "desks", since they cover the 169 countries with whom diplomatic relations exist and the other countries that do not have diplomatic relations (like China, Vietnam, North Korea, Saudi Arabia, etc.), as well as the international organisations.

This is the reason why some time ago, when an Ambassador told the Cardinal Secretary of State that he was honoured to serve at the number one diplomacy of the world, His Eminence replied: If ours is the first, I don't want to know what the second or third may be like!

Yet, permit me to say, that the results of the diplomatic activity of the Holy See in these last years have been noteworthy. Just to mention a few: the role of arbiter that the Holy See played between Argentina and Chile concerning the problem of the Beagle Canal that was leading to a war, but was settled with the "Tratado de Paz e Amistad", signed in the Vatican on November 19, 1983; the revision of the Lateran Concordat between Italy and the Holy See, signed on February 18, 1984 at Villa Madama; the signing of the atomic non-proliferation Treaty of 1971; the intense activity of the Holy See in favour of peace in Lebanon and between Israel and the Palestine Authority; the commitment that the Holy See made to assist in bringing about peace in the countries of ex-Yugoslavia, a commitment that was verified by the personal visit of Pope John Paul II to Sarajevo in 1996.

Moreover, let us recall the positive results in defence of life, the family and matrimony that were evident at the recent International Conferences in Rio de Janeiro, Cairo and Bejing. The interventions of Paul VI and John Paul II at the General Assembly of the United Nations have shown how the Holy See could be considered "the moral conscience" of the world today. In short, we can say that pontifical diplomacy serves the Pope not only in his pastoral ministry in favour of the Church, but also in his activity for the good of the international community.

In reality, precisely the fact that the Pope has a diplomatic represen-tation allows him to intervene in moments of tension and difficulties in favour of peace and the protection of human rights. One recalls the intense activity that Pope Pius XII undertook, through his Nuncios, during the Second World War to lead the conflicting nations to peace, to protect the prisoners of war and to aid those persecuted terribly at that time.

## V. WAYS AND MEANS OF THE INTERNATIONAL ACTIVITY OF THE HOLY SEE

After having shown the relationship between the Holy See and Vati-can City and the international subjectivity of the holy See, let us now turn to examine the means and the ways that the Holy See manifests itself on the international scene and the "interests" that she promotes.

Today, we speak often about "diplomacy in transition". Diplomacy in fact does change with the times. At the end of the last century, the foreign affairs of countries were intertwined between the courts and governments. Ambassadors were in a sense the makers of this policy. Today, the situation has changed. The rapid means of communications between the Capitals, democratisation of society, the phenomenon of globalisation, among others, have altered the chess-board of the national and international actors.

For example, national parliaments still have their importance, but they are more and more inspired by the recommendations and directives of the international parliamentary assemblies. Certainly, ambassadors are still indispensable in their role of representation and providing information, but the great political and economic events of today are conducted at the level of Heads of States who often meet directly. Let us take the United Nations as well, which despite the criticisms against it, still has its value and if it didn't exist, something similar would be created. Yet, world institutions like the World Bank, the International Monetary Fund and other regional ones which have power over the distribution of funds, obviously have acquired a certain weight in some political decisions. Even at the national level, Ministries, or as they are called in the United States "Departments" (like the Department of Health and Education, etc) which have the power to disburse funds, now must contend with non-governmental agencies which are in more direct contact with the people and which can yield much power in the mechanism of decision-making.

In a certain sense, this change of the international chess-board has also affected the way in which the Holy See makes its international presence known. Yes, it avails itself of a diplomatic corps to do so, but above all it does so through the person of Pope John Paul II who has brought the visibility of the papacy to a high level. It is the Pope with his travels, his interventions and his encounters who orientates the international activity of the Holy See.

Immediately after the fall of the Berlin wall, Fukuyama wrote a book entitled: "The End of History." It was a book that made a lot of noise at first. However, upon reflection one realises that not only has history not ended in its monotony, but, on the one hand, has actually entered into an exciting period of information, virtual reality and globalisation, and on the other hand, is marked by distressing tribal hatred and ethnic and nationalistic wars.

As such, someone who noted the Pope's contribution to the fall of the Berlin wall, predicted the end of his presence and his importance on the international scene. Yet, the contrary has taken place. From 1990 the Holy See has actually multiplied its diplomatic initiatives.

Taking into account the challenge that Samuel Huntington recognised in the inevitable "clash of civilisations", the Holy See promotes communication and dialogue among cultures, therefore tossing aside any reason that could lead to religious conflicts. Let's take the example of Russia where the Russian Orthodox Church has been embedded forever. This is upheld by the concept of "canonical territory", that is, Russia is inhabited primarily by orthodox believers and therefore, there is no room for other Churches there. This idea existed three, four centuries ago when Catholics and Protestants were "at war". Then something was realised: it is not territory that has rights, but people. If in a territory inhabited predominantly by the Orthodox, there are also Catholics or Lutherans or Anglicans, these people also have the right to receive spiritual assistance from their Churches which need to have the bare minimum of structures in order to fulfil their task. Therefore, it's not out of the question to push, if not to provoke, the Orthodox Church to respect fully the rights of other believers. For this reason the Catholic Church is not afraid of being accused of proselytism, because that is not what we are dealing with, but rather offering ministry to those who have a right to it.

As such, more and more numerous are the interventions of the Holy See in the international fora on subjects such as: international debt, migrants and refugees, humanitarian aid, distribution of land, disarmament, the environment, the rights of nations, extreme nationalism and savage capitalism.

What interests the Holy See above all is not Governments as such, but the people. This is the principle that guides the Holy See's position concerning international embargo. The Holy See does not exclude the validity of an embargo, but asks, and in this instance is supported by Russia, the United Nations to establish a precise mechanism to verify if an international sanction actually has an impact on a determined

Government and to decree its end when it is evident that it is only penalising the population, while the Government remains unpunished and intact.

This was the sense of the firmness of Pope John Paul II when he called for a review of the sanctions against Cuba. If after 37 years they have not reached their goal, that means that it is time to formulate a new approach that will move the Government, but not penalise the people.

On the other hand, we must remember that the Pope did not go to Cuba to preach an alternative political system. That is not his competence. Rather, he went to once again give courage and hope to the people of Cuba, so that they will have the strength to organise themselves and rebuild a society that respects their rights.

The diplomacy of the Holy See, as I said before, cannot and of course does not want to count on any military force, or for that matter economic power. Instead, it counts on the strength of conviction and of conscience. For this, it is a patient diplomacy, not accomplishing everything immediately, but calmly waiting for as long as it takes. In this sense, a Vatican expert of long ago was right when he wrote: "The Vatican thinks in terms of centuries."

BIBLIOGRAPHICAL REFERENCES

CARDIA, C. (ed.), *Vaticano e Santa Sede*, Bologna, Il Mulino, 1994, 347 p.

CARDINALE, I., *Le Saint-Siège et la Diplomatie. Aperçu historique, juridique et pratique de la Diplomatie Pontificale*, Paris, Desclée, 1962, 342 p.

CASAROLI, A., "Il Papato e le sfide del mondo moderno", in SCHULZ, W. and FELICIANI, G. (ed.), *Vitam impendere vero. Studi in onore di Pio Ciprotti*, Rome, Libreria Editrice Vaticana, 1986, 33-43.

CHELI, G., "La place et le rôle du Saint-Siège dans les institutions internationales", in D'ONORIO, J.-B. (ed.), *Le Saint-Siège dans les relations internationales*, Paris, Cerf, 1989, 87-100.

CIPROTTI, P, "La posizione internazionale della Santa Sede alla luce di recenti documenti inediti", *La comunità internazionale*, n. 3, 1974, p. 411 s.

DE RIEDMATTEN, H., "La presenza della Santa Sede negli organismi internazionali", *Concilium*, 1970, n° 8, p. 91 s.

D'ONORIO, J.-B., "Les concordats et conventions postconciliaires", in D'ONORIO, J.-B. (ed.), *Le Saint-Siège dans les relations internationales*, Paris, Cerf, 1989, 193-245.

DUPUY, A., *La Diplomatie du Saint-Siège après le IIe Concile du Vatican, le pontificat de Paul VI, 1963-1978*, Paris, Téqui, 1980, 343 p.

FERLITO, S., *L'attività internazionale della Santa Sede*, Milano, Giuffrè, 1988, 202 p.

FERLITO, S., "La Santa Sede e il mantenimento della pace: il caso del Beagle", *Il diritto ecclesiastico*, 1985, I, 60-97.

GALLINA, E., *Le organizzazioni internazionali e la Chiesa cattolica*, Rome, Studium, 1967, 222 p.

IRANI, G.E., *Santa Sede e Medio Oriente. Il ruolo del Papato nella controversia arabo-israeliana 1962-1988*, Milano, Vita e pensiero, 1990, VII + 217 p.

KÖCK, F.H., "La Santa Sede e la promozione dei diritti umani", in CONCETTI, G. (ed.), *I diritti umani. Dottrina e prassi*, Rome, Ed. A.V.E., 1982, 429-440.

LE TOURNEAU, D., "Les Legats Pontificaux dans le Code de 1983, vingt ans après la constitution apostolique 'Sollicitudo Omnium Ecclesiarum'", *Année canonique*, 1989, 229-260.

LEVILLAIN, PH. (ed.), *Dictionnaire historique de la Papauté*, Paris, Fayard, 1994, 1776 p.

OLIVERI, M., *The Representatives, the Real Nature and Function of Papal Legates*, Gerrards Cross, Van Duren, 1980, 192 p.

RULLI, G., "La Santa Sede e l'Onu", *La Civiltà Cattolica*, 1989, III, 154-158.

SCHULZ, W., "Lo Stato della Città del Vaticano e la Santa Sede, Alcune riflessioni attorno al loro rapporto giuridico", *Apollinaris*, 1978, 661-674.

# THE ROLE OF RELIGION IN THE
# ADVANCEMENT OF RELIGIOUS HUMAN RIGHTS

JAMES E. WOOD, JR.

This century has witnessed the emergence of the struggle for human rights throughout the world, and religious human rights lie at the heart of that struggle. By religious human rights are meant the inherent right of a person in public or in private to worship or not to worship according to one's own conscience, understanding, or preferences; to profess and to propagate one's faith; to join in association with others of like faith; and to change one's religious identity – all without hindrance, molestation, or discrimination. Religious human rights require the equality of all religions[1], as well as irreligion, before the law, and that, according to the law, a citizen neither enjoys advantages nor suffers disadvantages because of one's religious faith or identity.

The recognition of religious human rights as a valid principle in law has become one of those axiomatic commitments that is almost universally shared among the family of nations; this recognition is surely one of the major achievements of this century. While there is overwhelming evidence to indicate that religious human rights are far from being an existential reality in most of today's world, and nowhere fully realized, religious liberty has become a normative principle for most of the nations of the world and, conversely, the denial of religious liberty is almost everywhere viewed as morally and legally improper and unacceptable. Consequently, guarantees of religious rights and religious liberty presently appear in the vast majority of the national constitutions throughout the world today, including even totalitarian states and governments committed to atheistic communism. Although respect for religious human rights or religious liberty – namely the absence of discrimination based upon religion or belief and the equality of all religions before the law – can hardly be said to be descriptive of conditions as they exist in most countries of

---

[1] In the words of Lord Acton, "Religious liberty ... is possible only where the co-existence of different religions is admitted, with an equal right to govern themselves according to their own equal principles"; John Emerich Edward Dalberg-Acton, The *History of Freedom and Other Essays* (New York: Books for Libraries Press, 1967), 152.

the world today, there is profound significance to be found in the fact that the concept of religious liberty has come to have normative value almost universally.

Despite an almost universal commitment to religious human rights, as witnessed in the United Nations "Universal Declaration of Human Rights" in 1948[2], and, even more explicitly, in its "Declaration on the Elimination of All Forms of Intolerance and of Discrimination Based on Religion or Belief" in 1981[3], there is no universal consensus as to their intellectual or philosophical basis. While there are often important political and practical reasons for defending religious human rights, religious human rights need support of the major world religions themselves and should not depend primarily, let alone solely, on political expediency and self-interest considerations.

I

Guarantees of religious human rights, it should be noted, are a recent achievment in international law. As late as World War II, a worldwide study declared, "No writer asserts that there is a generally accepted postulate of international law that every State is under legal obligation to accord religious liberty within its jurisdiction[4]." Historically, the principle of religious human rights or religious liberty was rooted in the concept of "liberty of conscience," a phrase of modern origin that came into use after the sixteenth century and appeared most prominently during the seventeenth, eighteenth, and nineteenth centuries. Gradually, religious liberty was proclaimed to be both a natural and a divine right. Furthermore, it was reasoned, religious liberty required liberty of conscience. As John Milton expressed it, "Give me the liberty to know, to think, to believe, and to utter freely, according to conscience, above all other liberties[5]." In

---

[2] "Universal Declaration of Human Rights," G.A. Res. 217A(111) at 71, U.N. Dec.A/810 (1948) (entered into force 23 March 1976) [hereinafter Universal Declaration].

[3] G.A. Res. 36/55, U.N. GAOR, 36th Sess., Agenda Item 75, U.N. Doc. A/RES/36/55 (1981). The Declaration was adopted by unanimous consent by the U.N. General Assembly on 28 November 1981.

[4] Norman J. Padelford, *International Guarantees of Religious Liberty* (New York: International Misionary Council, 1942); quoted in M. Searle Bates, *Religious Liberty: An Inquiry* (New York: Harper and Brothers, 1945), 476.

[5] John Milton, *Areopagitica* (1644). In the words of the late Jacques Maritain, "With respect to the State, to the temporal community and to the temporal power ... freedom of conscience is a natural, inviolable right."

the words of the late Jacques Maritain, "With respect to the State, to the temporal community and to the temporal power ... freedom of conscience is a natural, inviolable right[6]."

Guarantees of religious human rights may be found in the norms of international law and by international agreements affirming these rights as an international standard among signatory nation-states, such as "The Universal Declaration of Human Rights" (1948)[7], "The International Covenant on Civil and Political Rights" (1966)[8], "The Principles of the Helsinki Final Act" (1975)[9], and "The Declaration on the Elimination of All Forms of Intolerance and of Discrimination Based on Religion or Belief" (1981)[10].

Although religious liberty was long advocated by individuals and religious dissenters, who at least sought religious freedom for themselves, full religious liberty was nowhere legally realized until the modern era and, even today, is far from being a reality in most of today's world. As late as World War II, one worldwide study declared, "No writer asserts that there is a generally accepted postulate of international law that every State is under legal obligation to accord religious liberty within its jurisdiction[11]." Today, the principle of religious human rights or religious liberty has come to be recognized as an accepted postulate in international law.

It is of profound historical significance that following the organization of the United Nations in 1945, concerted efforts were soon directed toward the formulation of Universal Declaration of Human Rights, including the principle of religious liberty as a fundamental right to which all member nations were to subscribe and in recognition of the vital relationship of religious liberty to relations between states. Recently, Professor Henry J. Steiner of Harvard Law School, observed that "no other document has so caught the historical moment, achieved the same moral and rhetorical force, or exerted so much influence on the [human rights] movement as a whole[12]." As is well known, one of the basic principles

---

[6] Jacques Maritain, *The Rights of Man and Natural Law* (New York: Scribner, 1943), 81-82 and notes.

[7] "Universal Declaration," supra, fn. 2.

[8] U.N. GAOR, 21 Sess., Supp. No. 16, at 71, U.N. Doc. A/6316) (entered into force 23 March 1976) [hereinafter ICCPR].

[9] "Conference on Security and Cooperation in Europe: Final Act (1975)"; reprinted in 14 I.L.M. 1923 (1975) [hereinafter Helskink Final Act].

[10] "Declaration on Religion and Belief," supra fn. 3.

[11] Padelford, *International Guarantees of Religious Liberty*, 17; quoted in Bates, *Religious Liberty: An Inquiry*, 476.

[12] "Securing Human Rights," *Harvard Magazine* (October 1998). Similarly, in *Pacem in Terris* (1962), Pope John XXIII praised the U.N. Universal Declaration as "an act of the highest importance" and "an important step forward on the path toward the juridico-political

included in the Charter of the United Nations is that of "the dignity and equality inherent in all human beings[13]." Therefore, all members nations "pledged themselves to take joint and separate action in cooperation with the Organization to promote and encourage universal respect for an observance of human rights and fundamental freedoms for all without distinction as to race, sex, language, or religion[14]."

Three years after its founding, the United Nations General Assembly adopted the "Universal Declaration of Human Rights[15]" in which it gave specific attention to a person's right to religion as a basic human right. Article 2 affirmed that everyone is to be entitled to all the rights and freedoms in the Declaration without respect to religion. Article 18 declared, "Everyone has the right to freedom of thought, conscience, and religion; this right includes freedom to change his religion or belief, and freedom, either alone or in community with others and in public or private, to manifest his religion or belief in teaching, practice, worship and observance." In various forms, this portion of the Declaration has been incorporated in the national constitutions of many nations, particularly in the nations' emerging since 1948.

After more than four decades of consultation and negotiation, the United Nations Assembly in November 1981 adopted the "Declaration on the Elimination of all Forms of Intolerance and of Discrimination Based on Religion or Belief[16]," in which the religious rights of the "Universal Declaration of Human Rights" were affirmed. In addition, the 1981 Declaration categorically declared that "no one shall be subject to discrimination by any State, institution, group of persons or person on grounds of religion or other beliefs[17]." Such discrimination, the Declaration went out of its way to note, must be regarded not only an "affront" to human dignity, but also a "disavowal" of the principles of the Charter of the United Nations and violation of the freedoms guaranteed in the "Universal Declaration of Human Rights." Thus, at long last, religious human rights were given explicit recognition in the family of nations as an inviolable and sacred human right.

organization of the world community." In his first encyclical, *Redemptor Hominis* (1979), Pope John Paul II spoke of it as a "magnificent effort" toward the establishment of the inviolable rights of persons, including religious freedom (No. 17), and in his address to the United Nations, 5 October 1995, he characterized the Universal Declaration as "one of the highest expressions of the human conscience of our time."

[13] U.N. Charter Art. 56.
[14] Ibid.
[15] Universal Declaration, supra fn. 2.
[16] Declaration on Religion or Belief, supra fn. 3.
[17] Ibid., Article 2.

It is well to remember that historically pleas for religious toleration and religious liberty have come primarily from religious minorities and dissenters, the religiously disenfranchised and persecuted, and not from religious majorities which enjoyed state patronage and support. At the same time, it should be noted, that the major advances toward the recognition of religious human rights and religious liberty in the modern world have come not from religious confessions of faith, ecclesiastical councils or synods, but from constitutions, legislative bodies, and courts of law. After the Middle Ages, the emergence of new nation-states and a new national spirit weakened the political power of old religious establishments to a degree from which they generally could not recover. In widely varying degrees, religious liberty became inexorably linked to the modern democratic state. In the twentieth century, among both the communities of faith and nation-states throughout the world, a broad consensus gradually evolved toward support of the principle of religious liberty, at least in some form.

Legal recognition of freedom of religion has been particularly aided, both in principle and in practice, by international relations that resulted in the ratification of treaties between states. As one major study on religious liberty written more than fifty years ago affirmed, "International law and religious liberty grew in intimate association[18]." The study found that a substantial majority of the writers of general treaties on international law following the time of Hugo Grotius (1583-1645), long recognized for his work as a codifier of international law, specifically referred to religious liberty in their documents. In the nineteenth century, with sovereign states identified with different religious traditions, it became common in the drawing up of treaties to include provisions granting the right of religious expression to the nationals of each contracting party in the territory of the other. Since these foreign nationals were identifiable by both their nationality and their religion, it was inevitable that specific safeguards came to be provided for freedom of conscience, worship, and religious work "upon the same terms as nationals of the state of residence," to use a phrase common to many of these international treaties with provisions of religious liberty.

There are many examples of the role of international agreement in the advance of religious human rights. The Treaty of Berlin in 1878 at the close of the Russo-Turkish War, with its provisions for the equal

---

[18] Bates, *Religious Liberty*, 476. From this study, Bates observed, "A review of the forty-seven writers of the more important treaties on international law, following the time of Hugo Grotius, shows that [a] full thirty refer to religious liberty"; ibid.

rights of religious minorities, has been called "the most important single expression of international agreement for religious liberty" prior to the post-World War I era[19]. Similar guarantees of religious liberty were embodied in the General Act relating to African Possessions[20] and the Minorities Treaties of 1919-23, following World War I[21]. Of special historical significance is the European Convention for the Protection of Human Rights and Fundamental Freedoms of 1953, which declared that "everyone has the right to freedom of thought, conscience, and religion[22]." Still later, thirty-five nation-states in 1975 signed the Helsinki Final Act (i.e., The Final Act of the Conference on Security and Cooperation in Europe) in which religious rights were made an integral part of a major international agreement between thirty-five nations of Europe, Canada, and the United States. Principle 7 of the document gives special attention to "respect for human rights and fundamental freedoms, including freedom of thought, conscience, religion, or belief[23]." Meanwhile, more and more states throughout the world voluntarily entered into constitutional and treaty commitments to secure religious liberty for their own citizens as well as for foreign residents. With the increasingly wide geographical distribution of adherents of the world's major religions, the religions themselves challenged those national policies' denying the religious rights of their adherents and communities of faith.

Indeed, the principle of religious liberty has increasingly become one of those axiomatic commitments that is almost universally recognized. In at least some modified form, the principle of religious liberty has come to be affirmed by virtually all national governments as a part of national law. Even if highly restrictive, some guarantees of religious liberty now appear in almost all national constitutions throughout the world[24].

[19] Ibid., 478.

[20] General Act of the Berlin Conference Respecting the Congo, 26 February 1885, 165 Consol. T.S. 485.

[21] See Richard B. Lillich and Hurst Hannum, *International Human Rights* (Buffalo, N.Y.: William S. Hein, 1995), 324.

[22] Convention for the Protection of Human Rights and Fundamental Freedoms, 4 November 1950, Article 9(1), 213 U.N.T.S. 222.

[23] Final Act, supra fn. 9, 1295.

[24] A somewhat random sampling well illustrates this among the following: EUROPE: Bulgaria (1991), "Freedom of conscience, freedom of thought, and choice of religious or atheistic views are inviolable" (Article 37); Germany (1991), "Freedom of faith, of conscience, and freedom of creed, religious or ideological (*weltanschaulich*), shall be inviolable" (Article 4); Russia (1991), "Establishes guarantees of the realization of human rights to freedom of conscience and freedom of religion" (Article 1 of The Soviet Law on

Nonetheless, religious liberty and respect for religious human rights remain far from realized in most of today's world. While freedom of religion is almost universally recognized de jure, the principle is by no means recognized de facto in most of today's world. Ironically, the very century that has witnessed the emergence of religious liberty and religious human rights as norms in international law and in most of the constitutions of the world has been the very century in which religious rights and religious freedom have been repeatedly and flagrantly violated on a wholesale scale throughout much of the world. For the first time in human history and for much of this century, numerous governments came into power with a sworn hostility to religion and expressly dedicated to the eradication of all religion.

Meanwhile, in more recent years, new democracies of both old and new nation-states have come into being which recognize freedom of religion as crucial to a democratic state. This is seen most recently in the emerging democracies of the New Europe. Throughout the New Europe, for example, constitutional reform commissions have been involved in addressing questions of freedom of religion and conscience, along with a broad range of other human rights. In some countries, permanent standing committees have been named by parliaments to address questions

Freedom of Conscience and Religion); Spain (1978), "Freedom of ideology, religion and worship of individuals and communities is guaranteed ..." (Article 16.1). AFRICA AND THE MIDDLE EAST: Algeria (1989), "Freedom of conscience and the freedom of opinion are inviolable" (Article 35); Egypt (1971), "The State shall guarantee the freedom of belief and the freedom of practice of religious rites" (Article 46); Israel (1949), Israel "will guarantee freedom of religion, conscience, language, education, and culture"; Nigeria (1979), "Every person shall be entitled to freedom of thought, conscience and religion" (Article 20); South Africa (1993), "Every person shall have the right to freedom of conscience, religion, thought, belief and opinion" (Article 14.1). ASIA AND OCEANIA: Australia (1986) "The Commonwealth shall not make any law for establishing any religion ... or for prohibiting the free exercise of any religion" (Chapter V); India (1950), "The State shall not discriminate any citizen on grounds only of religion" (Article 15.1); Indonesia (1945), "The State shall guarantee the freedom of the people to profess and to exercise their own religion" (Article 29.2); Japan (1947), "Freedom of religion is guaranteed to all" (Article 20); South Korea (1988), "All citizens shall enjoy freedom of conscience" (Article 19) and "All citizens shall enjoy freedom of religion" (Article 20.1); Sri Lanka (1945), "Every person is entitled to freedom of thought, conscience and religion" (Article 10). AMERICAS: Brazil (1988), "Freedom of conscience and of belief is inviolable" (Article 5.6); Canada (1982), "Everyone has ... freedom of conscience and religion" (Article 2); Chile (1980), Affirms "freedom of conscience, the manifestation of all beliefs, and the free exercise of all religions" (Article 19); Cuba (1992), "The State ... respects and guarantees the freedom of conscience and religion" (Article 55); Ecuador (1995), Affirms "freedom of conscience and religion, individually and collectively" (Article 19.5); Paraguay (1992), "Freedom of religion, worship, and ideology is hereby recognized without any restrictions other than those established in this Constitution and the law" (Article 24).

relating to new laws on religion on an ongoing basis. While there are many complex and difficult questions yet to be resolved in the face of counter forces of resistance, the subject of freedom of religion and conscience has become, as never before, a subject that is coming to be viewed, at least by some, as crucial to the movements of nations toward democracy and freedom. Among the questions inextricably intertwined with religious rights and religious liberty is one of ethnic and religious identity, which in many countries throughout the world is virtually conterminous with the rights of religious minorities.


II


All too often discussions of freedom of religion and conscience are virtually limited to the political restrictions imposed by government as if the problem is one simply between political or secular authority and religion. But the problem is also one deeply imbedded in the history of religion. From time immemorial, tolerance has not been characteristic of religion, quite to the contrary. Throughout human history, since religion generally served as the basis of the identity of a tribe, an ethnic community, or a nation, this religious identity formed the basis of differentiation from any other tribe, nation, or ethnic community, and from the world at large. What is more, religion often became the root cause of intergroup conflict between tribes, communities, and nations – for example, Israelites and Canaanites, Christians and Romans, Muslims and Jews, Eastern Orthodox and Roman Catholics, Sikhs and Hindus, Catholics and Protestants. In this way, religion fostered division and not unity, conflict and not concord, and at the heart of this division or conflict was each religion's perception of the truth, whether based upon its claims of prophetic revelation, some mystical experience(s), or a particular rational apprehension of existence. The very historical and metaphysical particularity of religion did not make for tolerance or the recognition of religious human rights outside of one's own religious tradition. Each religion claimed, or at least assumed, a uniqueness or superiority of its own, even when it maintained a posture of inclusivity and embraced some form of syncretism in its philosophical or theological propositions of truth.

To be sure, there have been historical incidents and teachings of tolerance in religious traditions, but they have been the exceptions and not the rule in the phenomenology of religion. Intolerance not tolerance,

conformity not nonconformity, and assent not dissent have been dominant motifs in the history of religions. More wars have been fought,
more persecutions have been carried out, and more lives have been lost
in the name of religion than probably for any other single cause. As one
historian has succinctly expressed it, "Nowhere does the name of God
and justice appear more frequently than on the banner and shield of the
conqueror[25]." Repeatedly, religious intolerance has been made the basis
of ethnic or racial prejudice and the rationale for political and social discrimination against nonadherents and nonconformists of the religious
establishment. Intrinsic to religion is the absoluteness of each religion's
perception of truth and the world. From his research as a historian of
religion, Gustav Mensching concluded that "all world religions raise an
extensive claim to absoluteness. Every one of them claims to be the only
true and valid faith and every one of them demands to be accepted as
such[26]." Through the centuries, the absoluteness of the truth embraced
by each religion provided a religious sanction of intolerance and discrimination.

The ultimate concerns of religious traditions have by and large pre-
cluded the tolerance of opposing views of faith and practice. "All religions are born absolute," Ernst Troeltsch observed, "because they follow
an unreflected compulsion and express a reality that demands recognition
and faith, not only for the sake of its existence, but more yet for the sake
of its validity[27]." The words of Jesus come to mind: "I am the way, the
truth, and the life; no man cometh to the Father, but by me[28]." This has
been true not only of the great Near Eastern faiths of prophetic revelation
(Judaism, Christianity, and Islam), which are by their very nature exclu-
sive in character, but also of the great Asian religions of mysticism and
rationalism (Hinduism, Buddhism, Confucianism, and Taoism), which
are inclusive in their perceptions of truth. Even among the latter, however, the claims of absoluteness are to be found. As Gautama Buddha
declared, "Having acquired enlightenment by myself, whom could I call
my teacher? I have no teacher, one like unto me is not to be found. In the
world with its *devas* (gods) there is no god equal to me[29]." One Buddhist

---

[25] Hubert Muller, *Religion and Freedom in the Modern World* (Chicago: University
of Chicago Press, 1963), 52.

[26] Gustav Mensching, *Tolerance and Truth in Religion* (University: The University of
Alabama Press, 1971), 152.

[27] Ernst Troelsch, *The Absoluteness of Christianity and the History of Religions* (Rich-
mond, Va.: John Knox Press, 1917), 138.

[28] *John* 14:6.

[29] Majjhima Nikaya 26.

text states, "There is no other way to gain salvation than through his [Buddha's] teaching[30]." While the causes or motives of religious intolerance are many and varied, they may be broadly summarized to include the following: a religion that is viewed as false and/or dangerous to the prevailing religious community; a religion that is perceived to be in conflict with the mores and moral values of a particular society; a religion that is judged to be subversive because its teachings threaten the pattern of political authority or the political policy being advanced; a religion that is believed to be alien to the culture in which it is being promulgated; or a religion that is identified with a foreign power.

The absoluteness of each religious tradition has served to provide a religious foundation for the intolerance of other faiths. From his years of study of religious persecution, the late Roland H. Bainton noted three prerequisites for religious persecution: "that the persecutor must believe that he is right"; "that the point in question is important"; and "that coercion will be effective[31]." Religious intolerance has been characterized by the absolutizing of the faith of the persecutor, the insistence of the persecutor on the necessity of defending his faith, fear of the consequences of tolerating moral and religious error, abhorrence of unorthodox views and practices, and intense hostility toward dissenters and nonconformists.

The religious identity of the nation has also made for political intolerance, since to be a dissenter in religion was to be an enemy of the state. The intolerance of ancient Israel toward foreign religious cults stemmed from their threat to the religious identity and unity of Israel, just as in ancient Greece to avow atheism was to manifest disloyalty to the state gods, and therefore atheism was met with court trials and legal action against such persons as adversaries of the state. As long as religion was the basis of the identity of the state, religion was an expression of patriotism and national loyalty. Any criticism of the religion of the state could, therefore, not be tolerated, since such criticism threatened the very foundation of the state. While unbelief represented a denial of the religious identity of the state, alien religious beliefs endangered the unity of the state or empire. This concern for the unity of the religious community was recognized throughout the ancient world and most of the history of the world. Because of the need to maintain the unity of the

---

[30] Yashomitra, *Commentary to Vasubhandu's Abhidharma-Kosha*; quoted in Mensching, *Tolerance and Truth in Religion*, 127.

[31] Roland H. Bainton, *The Travail of Religious Liberty* (Philadelphia: Westminster Press, 1951), 17.

nation or empire, religious differences or expressions of dissent were met with intolerance and even persecution. Diversity was abhorred, for it represented a threat to the unity and solidarity of the state.

In the history of religions, intolerance and persecution have not been restricted to any one era or to any one religion. Among numerous examples are: the persecution of the adherents of Amon of Ikhnaton (Ahmenhotep IV) by the religious establishment of Egypt; of the Canaanites by the Israelites; of Jesus and the early Christians by the Romans; of Buddhists by Shintoists; of Sufis by Orthodox Muslims; of heretics and Jews by Christians; of Muslims by Christians and Christians by Muslims; of Protestants by Catholics and of Catholics by Protestants; of Anabaptists by Lutherans; of sectarians by Eastern Orthodoxy and, indeed, by established churches generally; of "witches" and Quakers by Puritans in the Massachusetts Bay Colony; and of religious dissenters by religious establishments, as in present-day Iran. Among the religions of the world, tolerance has not been a characteristic in the phenomenon of religion...

The history of Christianity is replete with examples of the denial of toleration of dissenters who dared challenge the authority of the church or who embraced teachings in conflict with the church. Before the modern era, neither Roman Catholicism, nor Eastern Orthodoxy, nor Protestantism espoused toleration as such. Each tradition advocated coercion, even physical violence if necessary, to maintain its sway over the territories in which each became established. In the history of Christianity, as among other religions of the world, tolerance has not come easily. Tolerance toward other religions was generally deplored because it was viewed as being rooted in religious apathy and indifference.

## III

While freedom of religion and conscience has a long, albeit tortuous, history, voices against intolerance and respect for religious human rights may be traced back even to the ancient world. The practice of tolerance, however, emerged slowly. As alluded to earlier, there are, of course, examples of tolerance in the history of religions that should not be ignored. For example, the religious tolerance shown Jews in their years of Babylonian exile and their return to Jerusalem under Cyrus the Great.

The notion of tolerance and freedom of religion may be found in the teachings of the great world religions, even though it has been far less descriptive of the history of the religions themselves. In arguing the case for freedom of religion and conscience today, it should not be over-looked that there are explicit teachings of tolerance and condemnation of religious coercion and disrespect for religious views other than one's own to be found in the major world religions[32]. Furthermore, these teachings from the religions themselves stand to serve as helpful reminders to their adherents today that the sacred writings of their religious traditions' endorsing religious human rights may constitute a basis for interfaith relations based upon mutual respect and good will, even dialogue. In addition, these teachings provide support for constitutional and legal provisions on religious human rights that are being increasingly called for in both national and international law. Obviously, however, these teachings from the major world religions in support of religious human rights need to be lifted above the historical and nationalistic expressions of the religions themselves and to serve as a call to their adherents to be true to the ethical norms and teachings of their respective faiths with regard to freedom of religion and religious human rights[33].

In the ancient teachings of Hinduism, for example, intolerance and the very denigration of the religious rights of other faiths are expressly condemned. Basic to the Hindu tradition is the declaration, "Truth is

[32] Among recent publications that have highlighted this phenomenon, see: Leonard Swidler, *Religious Liberty and Human Rights in Nations and in Religions* (Philadelphia: Ecumenical Press, 1986); David Little, John Kelsay, and Abdulaziz Sachedina, *Human Rights and the Conflicts of Culture: Western and Islamic Perspectives on Religious Liberty* (Columbia: University of South Carolina Press, 1988); Arlene Swidler, ed., *Human Rights in Religious Traditions* (New York: Pilgrim Press, 1982); Leroy S. Rouner, *Human Rights and the World's Religions* (Notre Dame, Ind.: University of Notre Dame Press, 1988); Robert Traer, *Faith in Human Rights: Support in Religious Traditions for a Global Struggle* (Washington, D.C.: Georgetown University Press, 1991); Hans Küng and Jürgen Moltmann, eds., *The Ethics of World Religions and Human Rights* (Philadelphia: Trinity Press International, 1990); and David Cohn-Sherbok, ed., *World Religions and Human Liberation* (Maryknoll, N.Y.: Orbis Books, 1992).

[33] The purpose here in citing the teachings from the Sacred Writings of the major world religions bearing upon respect for religious human rights is not to suggest that there is an essential oneness among the major world religions in their concepts of ultimate reality or that they share a common world view or way of salvation. Rather, it should be understood that the selections from the sacred writings of the major world religions cited here are made solely because they reflect views of these traditions on religious human rights and the concept of religious liberty. As one Buddhist scholar, Phra Khantipolo, has rightly warned, "To try to steamroller every religion into the concept of basic sameness or 'all-is-one-ness' is to ignore facts in favor of a pre-conceived ideal." For, Kantipolo concludes, "in trying to believe in everything, one does in fact neither believe anything sincerely nor understand anything thoroughly"; see Phra Khantipolo, *Tolerance: Study from Buddhist Sources* (London: Rider, 1964), 35, 37.

One; sages call it by different names[34]". Or again, from Hindu Sacred Writings, "Ignorant is he who says, 'What I say and know is true; others are wrong.' It is because of this attitude of the ignorant that there have been doubts and misunderstandings about God. It is this attitude that causes dispute among men. But all doubts vanish when one gains self-control and attains tranquility by realizing the heart of Truth. Thereupon dispute, too, is at an end[35]." The ancient Sacred Writings of Hinduism affirm not only that tolerance and respect are to be shown those of other religious traditions, but also these writings reason that tolerance and respect are rooted in the belief that there is good to be found in all religions. "Like the bee, gathering honey from different flowers," Hindu Scriptures declare, "the wise man accepts the essence of different scriptures and sees only good in all religions[36]." In the words of one of Hinduism's most renowned twentieth-century thinkers and apologists, Sarvepalli Radhakrishnan, "The faiths of others all desire to be honoured for one reason or another. By honouring them, one exalts one's own faith and at the same time performs a service to the faith of others. By acting otherwise, one injures one's own faith and also does disservice to that of others. For if a man extols his own faith and disparages another, because of devotion to his own and because he wants to glorify it, he seriously injures his own faith[37]."

Similarly, the tolerance of Buddhism, the first of the great world religions to become international, was demonstrated in its encounters with other faiths. In China and Japan, where the geographical outreach of Buddhism resulted in its becoming thoroughly indigenous to those cultures, Buddhism by and large sustained a harmonious coexistence with the national faiths of both countries with little conflict and discord on its part. "Buddhism was and is, on the whole, an outspokenly tolerant religion; this is documented by the fact that wherever it has spread it has never tried to annihilate the original religion, but rather has existed beside it …[38] Buddhism is deeply rooted in the concept of religious freedom and respect for religious human rights. A charitable attitude toward all religious views and their adherents is encouraged. The founder of Buddhism, Siddhartha Gautama, urged that his followers not bear ill-will

---

[34] *Rig Veda* Book 1, Hymn 164:46.
[35] *Srimad Bhagavatam* 11:15.
[36] Ibid., 11:3.
[37] S. Radhakrishnan, *Religion in a Changing World* (London: George Allen and Unwin, Ltd., 1967), 174.
[38] Mensching, *Tolerance and Truth in Religion*, 22.

toward anyone who spoke ill of him. Rather, Gautama declared, "If anyone were to speak ill of me or my doctrine or my Order, do not bear ill-
will towards him, do not be upset or perturbed at heart; for if you were
to be so, it will only cause *you* harm[39]." Again, to quote from Buddhist
Scriptures, "The Buddha says, 'To be attached to a certain view and to
look down upon other views as inferior – this the wise men call a fetter
[i.e., a wrong].'[40]" In teaching respect for all believers, Gautama
declared, "If a man says 'This is my faith,' so far he maintains truth. But
by that he cannot proceed to the absolute conclusion: 'This alone is
Truth, and everything else is false.'[41]" In the Sacred Writings of one
Buddhist sect in Japan, the Omoto Kyo, is to be found the following:
"There is not a single place in all the corners of the world where God is
absent[42]." The first of the great world religions to become international,
Buddhism has demonstrated throughout much of its history a spirit of
tolerance and a respect for religious human rights in its encounters with
other faiths.

Still other ancient religious traditions call for respect to be shown
toward those of other faiths. In the Scriptures of Jainism, founded like
Buddhism six centuries before the dawn of Christianity, appears the following: "Those who praise their own doctrines and disparage the doctrines of others do not solve any problem[43]." Jains are admonished in
their sacred scriptures to "comprehend one philosophical view through
comprehensive study of another one[44]." This regard for other religious
traditions is affirmed also in Confucianism. "In the world there are
many different roads," Confucius said, "but the destination is the same.
There are a hundred deliberations but the result is one[45]."

The tradition of Judaism has long contended for religious human
rights. In Judaism, the very covenant which God established with Israel
affirmed that God's love is for all people, and purposed that through that
covenant, "All the families of the earth are to be blessed[46]." In the Holy
Scriptures of Judaism, which are, of course, also viewed as Sacred
Scripture in the Christian tradition, are these words: "For from the ris-
ing of the sun to its setting my name is great among the nations, and in

---

[39] *Digha Nikaya* 1:3.
[40] *Sutta Nipata* 798.
[41] *Majjhima Nikaya* 2:176.
[42] *Michi-no-Shiori*.
[43] *Sutrakritanga* 1.1:50.
[44] *Acarangasutra* 5:113.
[45] *I Ching*, 2:5.
[46] *Genesis* 12:3.

every place incense is offered to my name, and a pure offering; for my name is great among the nations, says the Lord of hosts[47]." In the *Tosefta*, Rabbi Joshua is recorded as saying, "There are righteous men among the nations who have a share in the world to come[48]." The ultimate ground for respect for all human rights in Judaism is to be found in its teachings concerning the infinite worth of every person or the sanctity of every individual life. Respect for divergent faiths is clearly and explicitly affirmed in the Talmudic writings of Judaism, as illustrated by the following: "The scholars ... sit in groups; some forbid and others permit; some declare a thing unclean and others declare it clean; some pronounce a thing unfit and others pronounce it fit. Lest anyone say to them I shall sit back and not study, Scripture declares, 'They are given from one shepherd: one God created them, one leader gave them, the Master of all things uttered them!' Thou, too, therefore, make thine ear like a hopper and take in the words of them that pronounce unfit and the words of them that pronounce fit[49]." In the Mishnah are to be found these words, "Therefore, was a single person [first] created to teach thee that if anyone destroys a single soul ... Scripture charges him as though he had destroyed a whole world, and whosoever rescues a single soul ... Scripture credits him as though he had saved a whole world ... The Holy One has stamped all mankind with the die of the first man and yet not one of them is like to his fellow. Therefore, everyone is bound to say, 'For my sake was the universe created.'[50]" One of Judaism's most beloved and respected scholars in this century, the late Rabbi Abraham Heschel, was fond of saying, "God's voice speaks in many languages" – a view widely shared in Judaism[51]. For centuries, the missionary motive has been largely disavowed by Judaism as incompatible with religious tolerance. Teachings of tolerance toward other faiths also have a long history in Christianity. Jesus preached against intolerance and religious bigotry[52]. In Christianity, religious tolerance and the sanctity of religious rights may be found, as with Judaism, in the affirmation that all of humanity is created in the image of God. Beyond that, Christian

---

[47] *Malachi* 1:11.

[48] *Tosefta Sanhedrin*, 13.2.

[49] Judah Goldin, *The Living Talmud: The Wisdom of the Fathers and Its Classical Commentaries* (Chicago: University of Chicago Press, 1957), 21.

[50] *M. Sanhedrin*, 4:5.

[51] Abraham Joshua Heschel, *God in Search of Man: A Philosophy of Judaism* (New York: The Jewish Publication Society of America, 1955), 142.

[52] For some examples of Jesus' teachings against religious intolerance and religious bigotry, note the following: Mathew 8:5 ff., 9:10-13, 21:12-45, 23:1-39; Luke 7:31-50, 9:51-56, 10:25-37, 15:1-32; and John 4:7 ff. 21, 24, 46 ff.

Scripture categorically declares that "God has not left himself without witness[53]" and speaks of "the true Light, which lighteth *every* man that cometh into the world[54]." Religious tolerance and respect for religious rights may be found also in Christian Scripture in the manner of God's dealings with all human beings. Peter, one of the disciples of Jesus who became a leader of early Christianity, is quoted as saying, "God has shown me that I should not call any one common or unclean." "Truly I perceive that God shows no partiality, but in every nation any one who fears him and does what is right is acceptable to him[55]." Between Jews and Gentiles, Paul also declared, "God shows no partiality[56]." A person's capacity for freedom, the Scripture maintains, is from God. As Paul wrote, "Where the spirit of the Lord is present, there is freedom[57]." The very invitation of Jesus throughout the Gospels is repeatedly conditioned with the words, "whosoever will ..." or "if you want to... [58]," words which by their very nature constitute an invitation born out of respect for the human will in matters of religious belief. God's very approach to all of humankind is perhaps nowhere in Christian Scripture more clearly portrayed than in the last book of the New Testament, *The Revelation*, in which respect for the inviolability of the religious rights of every person is presented dramatically and unequivocally: "Behold I stand at the door and knock; if *any* person hears my voice and opens the door, I will come into his house and eat with him, and he will eat with me[59]."

In the third century, Tertullian wrote that freedom of religion "is a human right, a privilege of nature ... everyone should worship as he pleases[60]." Almost a century later, Lactantius argued that "nothing is as much a matter of freewill as religion ... It is religion alone in which freedom has planted her dwelling. For beyond everything else it is a question of freewill[61]." Unfortunately, pleas for religious toleration, not to mention religious liberty, have with rare exception come from persecuted minorities and the religiously disenfranchised rather than communities of faith of social status and political power. While long advocated

---

[53] *Acts* 14:17.

[54] *John* 1:9.

[55] *Acts* 10:34-35.

[56] *Romans* 2:11.

[57] *2 Corinthians* 3:17.

[58] See, for example, *Matthew* 19:21-22.

[59] *The Revelation* 3:20.

[60] Quoted in Arnold Toynbee, ed., *The Crucible of Christianity: Judaism, Hellenism, and the Background to the Christian Faith* (New York: World Publishing Co., 1969), 350.

[61] Lactantius, Epitome, 54.

by individuals such as Marsilius of Padua in Italy and by various religious minorities, religious liberty was not widely realized until the modern era, and, even today, is by no means universally enjoyed.

In Islam, the Qur'an categorically declares that "there shall be no compulsion in religion[62]." The Qur'an further declares that belief is ultimately a matter of personal choice: "Proclaim, O Prophet, This is the truth from your Lord; then let him who will, believe, and let who will, disbelieve[63]." Tolerance toward other religions is explicitly enjoined on those who follow the Qur'an, as follows: "Revile not those deities whom the unbelievers call upon and worship[64]." Indeed, according to the teachings of the Qur'an, Muslims can respect the believers and the teachings of all religions – even those not mentioned in the Qur'an, such as Hinduism, Buddhism, Jainism, and Confucianism[65]. According to Islam, a person's freedom to choose is prerequisite to faith. Again, in the words of the Qur'an, "If it had been the Lord's will, all the people on the earth would have come to believe, one and all. Are you then going to compel the people to believe except by God's dispensation?"[66]

Similar teachings may be found in Scriptures of Sikhism, whose founder, Nanak, declared, "Search not for the True One afar off; He is in every heart[67]." According to Sikhism, people of God are to be found in all religions. The Scriptures of Sikhism declare, "There are those who read the Vedas and others – Christians, Jews, Muslims – who read the Semitic scriptures. Some wear blue, some white robes. Some call themselves Muslims, others Hindus. Some aspire to *bahishat* [Muslim heaven], some to *swarga* [Hindu heaven]. Says Nanak, Whoever realizes the will of the Lord, he will find out the Lord's secrets[68]!"

While these citations from the teachings of the religions hold special significance in establishing a linkage between the history of religion and religious human rights, at the same time, it must once again also be acknowledged that the spirit of tolerance and respect for religious human rights have not, by any means, been historically characteristic or descriptive of the religions themselves. Alas, none of the world religions has

---

[62] *Qur'an* 2:256.

[63] Ibid., 18:29.

[64] Ibid., 6:108.

[65] See *Qur'an* 35:24; 40:78; and 22:67.

[66] Ibid., 10:99-100; still another translation given ends with these words: "Wilt thou then compel mankind against their will, to believe?"

[67] M. A. MacAuliffe, *The Sikh Religion: Its Gurus, Sacred Writings, and Anthems*, 6 vols. (Oxford: Clarendon Press, 1909), 1:328.

[68] *Adi Granth, Rag Ramkali*, 885.

lived up to its own teachings with regard to freedom of religion and con-science[69]. This is readily observable in the history of Christianity, not only with respect to religious human rights, but also with respect to its original teachings on peace and its repudiation of the use the sword or violence. The disparity between the teachings of the religions and their historical expression is simply undeniable. This disparity between faith and practice has plagued all of the world religions, which, without exception, have all too often been but pale shadows, sometimes even perversions, of their true essence. As alluded to earlier, the historical record of the religions has often been one of contradiction to their teach-ings. Admittedly, the sanctity of the rights of the individual person and the basic human right to religious self-identity have been flagrantly and repeatedly violated by the religions themselves. In fact, as alluded to ear-lier, the hallmarks of the history of religion have been intolerance not tolerance, conformity not nonconformity, and assent and not dissent.

It cannot be denied, for example, that for more than a thousand years the history of Christianity was marked by intense intolerance and perse-cution of Jews and all religious dissenters, who were readily branded as "heretics." Nevertheless, despite any disparity between the history of religions and their sacred writings, special importance must be given to the presence of the concept of religious human rights in the scriptures of the major religions themselves, since these writings provide for each of the religious traditions the authoritative teaching norms of the faith. Even from this brief sampling, there are clearly valuable resources to be found in the great world religions to show that the concept of religious human rights, far from being an alien concept, is expressly endorsed within the very core of the teachings of the major world religions.

IV

Freedom of religion and conscience may not only be found in the sacred writings of the major religions of the world, but is also rooted in the nature of religion. The reality is that religious intolerance is antithet-ical to the nature of religion and is, indeed, religion's worst enemy. To

---

[69] There are those who would readily cite passages in the Scriptures of Judaism, Christianity, and Islam, in particular, that would appear to be contradictory to showing respect or even tolerance toward those of other religious traditions. The point being made here, however, is that there are sacred writings of the world's religions that do affirm a respect for the religious rights of others.

believe is a *voluntary* act. To be true to itself, authentic religion must wait upon the voluntary responses of persons who are free of coercion in order for religious faith to be genuine and to be true to itself. Recognition of this was conceded by the early church fathers. Near the close of the second century, Justin Martyr, who argued for the principle of the *logos spermatikos*, namely that the seed of the divine word is also present outside of the Christian tradition, perceptively wrote, "Nothing is more contrary to religion than constraint[70]." In the third century, when Emperor Septimus Severus issued a decree in 202 forbidding conversion to Christianity, Tertullian wrote that freedom of religion is a fundamental right. "It is a matter of both human and natural law," he declared, "that every man can worship as he pleases ... It is not in the nature of religion to impose itself by force," but "should be adopted freely[71]." Almost a century later, and with considerable insight into the nature of religion, Athanasius declared, "It is not with the sword and spear, nor with soldiers and armed force that truth is to be propagated, but by counsel and sweet persuasion[72]." Similarly, Lactantius, the tutor of Emperor Constantine's son, argued that "it is only in religion that liberty has chosen to dwell. For nothing is so much a matter of free will as religion, and no one can be required to worship what he does not will to worship. He can perhaps pretend, but he cannot will[73]."

During the Middle Ages, when religious liberty existed nowhere in Europe, Marsilius of Padua, a Catholic lawyer, eloquently argued in the fourteenth century that coercion is completely foreign to the nature of religion and that religious convictions by their very nature cannot be forced. No religious authority has the right to exercise coercion for compliance to religious commandments. "For it would be useless," Marsilius wrote, "for him to coerce anyone to observe them, since the person who observed them under coercion would be helped not at all toward eternal salvation[74]." "For Christ did not ordain that anyone should be coerced to observe in this world the law made by him, and for this reason he did not appoint in this world a judge having coercive power over

---

[70] Quoted in M. Searle Bates, *Religious Liberty: An Inquiry* (New York: Harper and Brothers, 1945), 137.

[71] *Ad Scapulam*, 2; Migne, *Patrologia Latina*, 1:699; quoted in Joseph Lecler, S.J., "Religious Freedom: An Historical Survey," in *Religious Freedom*, ed. Neophytos Edelby and Teodoro Jimenez-Urresti, Concilium (New York: Paulist Press, 1966), 5.

[72] *Divina Instituta*, 54; Migne, *Patrologia Latina*, 6:1061.

[73] Lactantius, *Divina Instituta*, 1,5c 20; Migne, *Patrologia Latina*, 6:516.54.

[74] Marsilius, *Defensor Pacis*, trans. Alan Gewirth (New York: Columbia University Press, 1956), II,ix,2.

transgressors of his law[75]." "Even if it were given to the bishop or priest
to coerce men in those matters which relate to divine law, it would be
useless. For those who were thus coerced would not be helped at all
toward eternal salvation by such compulsion[76]." As with earlier voices
for religious liberty, Marsilius espoused religious liberty as a matter of
principle and viewed religious liberty as an essential feature of authentic
religion.

Two centuries later, Desiderius Erasmus, the great Catholic humanist
and irenicist, wrote similarly that the use of coercion is contrary to the
nature of religion and, therefore, he argued for "the futility of persecution[77]." In a letter to John Carondolet, Erasmus wrote, "When faith is in
the mouth rather than in the heart, when the solid knowledge of Sacred
Scripture fails us, nevertheless by terrorization we drive men to believe
what they do not believe, to love what they do not love, to know what
they do not know. That which is forced cannot be sincere, and that
which is not voluntary cannot please Christ[78]."

Special tribute must always be given to the Radical Reformers who
championed voluntarism in religion and its corollary the separation of
church and state, that is the separation of religious affairs from temporal
power and the denial of the use of temporal power in religious matters[79].
The voices of the Radical Reformation for religious liberty were predi-
cated upon the uncoerced response to the gospel. This, they held, was
essential for the *esse* of the true church. Thus, the use of coercion in

---

[75] Ibid.

[76] Ibid., II, v,6.

[77] Quoted in Roland H. Bainton, *Erasmus of Christendom* (New York: Charles Scribner's Sons, 1969), 185.

[78] *Ep.* 1334, 5 January 1523, in *Opus epistolarum*, 5:11.362-81; quoted in *Concerning Heretics: Whether They Are To Be Persecuted and How They Are To Be Treated: A
Collection of the Opinions of Learned Men, Both Ancient and Modern*, ed. Sebastian
Castellio and trans. Roland H. Bainton (New York: Columbia University Press, 1935),
34. Later in 1519, in response to Martin Luther's dramatic public challenge at Wittenberg
of the Roman Catholic Church, Erasmus wrote to the archbishop of Mainz, the following:
"If he is innocent, I would not like to see him crushed by evil factions; if he is in error, I
would like to see him cured, not lost. Such conduct would agree better with the example
of Christ who ... did not extinguish the smoking flax, nor break the bruised reed"; quoted
in Joseph Lecler, S.J., *Toleration and Reformation*, trans. T. L. Westow, 2 vols. (New
York: Association Press, 1960), 1:116.

[79] In his monumental study of the Radical Reformation, George H. Williams concluded that "almost all of the Radicals [i.e., Radical Reformers] insisted on the utter separation of the church from the state and found in the willingness of the Magisterial
Reformers [e.g., Martin Luther, Huldreich Zwingli, and John Calvin] to use coercive
power of princes, kings, and town councilors an aberration from apostolic Christianity no
less grievous than papal pretensions"; see Williams's *The Radical Reformation* (Philadelphia: The Westminster Press, 1962), 860.

religion was opposed. "A Turk or a heretic," Balthasar Hubmaier wrote, "is not convinced by our act, either by the sword or with fire, but only with patience and prayer; and so we should await with patience the judgment of God[80]."

Writing a century later in England, in a book which boldly set forth for the first time in the English language the right of universal religious liberty, Thomas Helwys argued that the nature of religion removed it from the jurisdiction of the civil ruler.

"Our Lord the King is but an earthly King, and he hath no authority as a King, but in earthly causes, and if the Kings people be obedient & true subjects, obeying all humane lawes made by the King, our Lord the King can require no more: for men's religion to God, is betwixt God and themselves; the King shall not answere for it, neither may the King be jugd betwene God and Man. Let them be heretikes, Turks, Jewes, or whatsoever it apperteynes not to the earthly power to punish them in the least measure[81]."

Similarly, a few years later, Leonard Busher of England, wrote also in opposition to the use of temporal power in religion: "It is not only unmerciful, but unnatural and abominable, yea, monstrous, for one Christian to vex and destroy another for difference and questions of religion[82]."

The voluntariness of religious faith has come to be increasingly recognized in contemporary thought[83]. Reaffirmation of the voluntary character of religion has been clearly affirmed, for example, in twentieth-century Christian ecumenical thought. The World Council of Churches has on various occasions seen religious liberty as integral to the nature of religion and religious faith. "God's redemptive dealing with men is not coercive. Accordingly, human attempts by legal enactment or by pressure of social custom to coerce or eliminate faith are violations of the fundamental ways of God with men. The freedom which God has

---

[80] Henry C. Vedder, *Balthasar Hubmaier* (New York: G. P. Putnam's Sons, 1905), 86; see also Article 16 of "On Heretics and Those Who Burn Them," in *Balthasar Hubmaier: Theologian of Anabaptism*, trans. and ed. H. Wayne Pipkin and John H. Yoder (Scottdale, Penn.: Herald Press, 1989), 62.

[81] Thomas Helwys, *A Short Declaration of the Mistery of Iniquity*, fac. reprint ed. (London: Kingsgate Press, 1935), 69.

[82] *Religious Peace or a Plea for Liberty of Conscience*; quoted in Anson Phelps Stokes, *Church and State in the United States*, 3 vols. (New York: Harper and Brothers, 1950), 1:113.

[83] See James E. Wood, Jr., "Religious Liberty in Ecumenical and International Perspective," *Journal of Church and State* 10 (Autumn 1968): 421-36.

given ... implies a free response to God's love ... [84]" In the words of
Vatican II, "God calls men to serve him in spirit and in truth; hence they
are bound in conscience, but they stand under no compulsion[85]."

The heart of the matter is that for religion to be authentic, it must be
a voluntary, personal, and free act, and membership in a faith community is one of voluntary association. Faith is not faith if its voluntary
character is abridged by coercion. As Augustin Leonard, a Catholic theologian, wrote, "An imposed faith is a contradiction in terms ... faith
must be free if it is not to destroy itself[86]." Recognition of religious liberty is fundamental to religious human rights and, indeed, to all other
human rights. In the words of the late A. F. Carrillo de Albornoz, for
some years the Secretary of the Secretariat on Religious Liberty of the
World Council of Churches, "No intellectual ingenuity, no organized
institution, no kind of compulsion and no power of persuasion can
change the fact that God deals with men as free and responsible beings
and that he expects from them an uncoerced response[87]." Or, as Albert
Hartmann expressed it, "A person's one and only means of learning
God's will is the voice of one's conscience[88]." The right to religious
identity and to a personal religious faith, including association with others of like faith, requires voluntariness. Religious human rights are
thereby undermined and vitiated whenever any form of external coercion
is superimposed on the individual.


V


The problem of religious tolerance is clearly "one of the great and
most urgent challenges now confronting the world[89]." The action taken
by the United Nations General Assembly, 25 November 1981, in adopting

---

[84] "Statement on Religious Liberty," in *The New Delhi Report: The Third Assembly
of the World Council of Churches, 1961* (New York: Association Press, 1962), 159.

[85] *De Libertate Religiosa: A Declaration of Religious Freedom; see The Documents
of Vatican II: All Sixteen Official Texts Promulgated by the Ecumenical Council, 1963-
1965*, ed. Walter M. Abbott, S.J. and trans. Joseph Gallagher (New York: Guild Press,
1966), 690.

[86] Augustin Leonard, "Freedom of Faith and Civil Toleration," in *Tolerance and the
Catholic* (New York: Sheed and Ward, 1955), 113.

[87] A. F. Carrillo de Albornoz, *The Basis of Religious Liberty* (New York: Association
Press, 1963), 74.

[88] Albert Hartmann, *Toleranz und Christlicher Glaube* (Frankurt-am-Main: Knecht,
1955), 5.

[89] Mensching, *Tolerance and Truth in Religion*, 10.

the "Declaration on the Elimination of All Forms of Intolerance and of Discrimination Based on Religion or Belief," while long overdue, was an important step taken by the family of nations[90]. Adopted first by the Commission on Human Rights in March 1981, the action taken by the United Nations Assembly followed twenty years of negotiations. Although there are serious limitations in the Declaration itself with respect to the omission of certain basic religious rights, the Declaration deserves the strong support of all religious faiths. In fact, the religions of the world should lead the way in calling for a convention to expand the Declaration and include some of those provisions now presently omitted: the equal protection of all religions or the right of judicial review when one's religious rights are denied; the freedom to witness to one's faith in public life; the freedom to disseminate the teachings of one's faith; the freedom of religious association on a local and national basis; and the freedom to maintain, without unwarranted restrictions, relationship with one's religious community at the international level.

This is an age of religious encounter, when new and old religious faiths can no longer remain isolated from one another or ignore each other's presence in today's world. This religious encounter is accentuated by a world that has increasingly come to be perceived as a "global village," one in which distances halfway around the globe are measured by only a few hours of jet travel. At the same time, through immigration and missionary outreach, the geographical distribution of the major world religions, as well as many new religions, has reached worldwide dimensions. International travel, international cultural exchange, and international relations through trade and treaty negotiations have contributed significantly to interreligious encounter and thereby have further underscored the need for the commitment of nations to uphold religious human rights. To express it another way, legal recognition of freedom of religion and conscience has become an international necessity.

The international dimension of contemporary life enjoins all religious faiths to espouse religious liberty for all persons throughout the world. As the World Council of Churches affirmed at its First Assembly in Amsterdam more than thirty-five years ago: "An essential element in a good international order is freedom of religion ... Christians, therefore, view the question of religious freedom as an international problem. They are concerned that religious liberty be everywhere secured. In pleading

---

[90] See the author's essay, "The Proposed United Nations Declaration on Religious Liberty," *Journal of Church and State* 23 (Autumn 1981): 413-22. The "Declaration" is printed in full at the conclusion of this essay.

for this freedom, they do not ask for any privilege to be granted to Christians that is denied to others[91]." Almost twenty years ago, Vatican II declared: "In view of the increasing international relations between people of different cultures and religions and for the establishment and strengthening of peaceful relations and concord in the human family, it is necessary that throughout the world religious liberty should be provided with effective legal safeguards and the supreme duty and right of man freely to lead a religious life in society should be observed[92]." Or, as Pope John Paul II has declared, "The limitation of the religious freedom of individuals and communities not only is a painful experience for them, but above all strikes at man's very dignity, regardless of the religion professed ... [93]" The religions of the world must come to recognize that the denial of religious liberty to any one group is a threat to the religious liberty of all, and that to abridge the religious rights of any one religious adherent is to imperil the rights of all religious adherents.

The defense of religious liberty is a defense of the religious dimension of human experience and of the integrity of liberty of conscience in matters of religious belief and commitment. For the religions of the world, the denial of religious liberty must come to be seen as incompatible with authentic religious experience. Coercion in religion is antithetical to genuine religious commitment and religious faith. Writing during the middle of the seventeenth century, Roger Williams observed that the greatest danger of state sponsorship of religion is hypocrisy, "which turns and dulls the edge of all conscience either toward God or man," a result of trying to compel belief[94]. A century later, John Locke wrote that religious persecution serves to make "men worse hyprocrites than they were before, by a new act of hypocrisy" and thereby "to corrupt the manners of the rest of the church[95]." Freedom of religion, in the words of John Oman, makes "honest religion" possible[96]. Or, as Robert Lawson

---

[91] W.A. Visser' T. Hooft, ed., *The First Assembly of the World Council of Churches*: Held at Amsterdam, August 22-September 4, 1948 (New York: Harper and Brothers, 1949), 97.

[92] *De Libertate Religiosa*, 7 December 1965.

[93] From an address delivered by John Paul II, 10 March 1984, in the Fifth International Colloquium on Juridical Studies, sponsored by the Pontifical Lateran University, Rome, Italy.

[94] *Complete Writings of Roger Williams* (New York: Russell and Russell, 1963), 7:181.

[95] John Locke, "A Third Letter of Toleration": in *Works*, 10 vols. (London: Thomas Tegg, 1823; reprinted in Germany: Scientia Verlag Aalen, 1963), 6:379; cf. 147, 395.

[96] Quoted in Robert Lawson Slater, *World Religions and World Community* (New York: Columbia University Press, 1963), 223.

Slater has written, "Freedom of religion is essential to genuine religion or sincere religious conviction[97]." Freedom of religion is also in the interest of the state since religion is thereby assured that it may function in society without depending on political means or being made to serve political ends.

As never before, the religions of the world need to lead the way in their renunciation of intolerance and religious discrimination, both in principle and in practice. The call today to genuine tolerance must be sounded by the religions themselves. Let it be understood that tolerance is not in conflict with the truths affirmed by the religions of the world, for tolerance does not mean the absence of personal belief or commitment, but rather genuine regard for authentic religious expression among other faiths and their pilgrims. Tolerance does require that the religions of the world take each other seriously and respect the integrity of other religious traditions. While, to be sure, the world's religions need to move beyond mere tolerance, or even good will, to genuine interfaith dialogue and avowed support of religious liberty, tolerance is prerequisite to any genuine interfaith dialogue and avowed support of religious human rights. An important place for each religious tradition to begin is the development of a religious foundation for tolerance and for religious liberty, in which pluralism of religious faiths is acknowledged and freedom of religion is espoused.

The growing recognition of religious liberty in international law was accompanied by broad ecumenical endorsements of religious liberty by the churches. With the convening of the First Assembly of the World Council of Churches in Amsterdam in 1948, a clear voice for religious rights and religious liberty was sounded in a document titled, "Declaration on Religious Liberty." The Declaration called on the churches "to support every endeavor to secure within an international bill of rights adequate safeguards for freedom of religion and conscience, including the right of all men to hold and change their faith, to exercise it in worship and practice, to teach and persuade others, and to decide on the religious education of their children." The Declaration further asserted that religious liberty is "an essential element in a good international order ... [that] should be secured everywhere. In pleading for this freedom, the Declaration declared, "[Christians] ... do not ask for any privilege to be granted to Christians that is denied to others[98]." Adopted unanimously,

[97] Ibid., 222.
[98] W. A. Visser 't Hooft, ed., *The First Assembly of the World Council of Churches: Held at Amsterdam, August 22-September 4, 1948* (New York: Harper and Brothers, 1949), 93-95.

the Amsterdam Declaration remains a landmark in the history of religious liberty and must be credited with having exerted some influence on the final adoption a few months later of the "Universal Declaration of Human Rights" by the United Nations.

Subsequent assemblies of the World Council of Churches have not only reaffirmed the Amsterdam Declaration but have continued to give voice to the Council's commitment to religious rights and religious liberty. Likewise, the endorsement of religious liberty by the Roman Catholic Church in Vatican II remains a significant chapter in the advancement of religious human rights. Affirming both the natural right of corporate religious freedom as well as individual religious freedom, Vatican II declared that "the right to religious freedom has its foundation in the very dignity of the human person" and that a person "should not be coerced to act against his own conscience, nor be impeded to act according to this conscience" and religious communities "have the right not to be hindered from publicly teaching and testifying to their faith both by the written and the spoken word[99]."

At a time, in the words of Vatican II, "The human race is becoming more clearly united and ties between different peoples are becoming stronger[100]," the role of religion in the building of a world community has become a crucial issue for the future of mankind. In a world made smaller through advances in communications and travel, the interdependence of nations and societies is inescapable, but whether or not a basis for world community can be established is yet to be resolved. This much is clear: the role of religion is central in the advancement of religious liberty and world peace and in the development of a world community if civilization is to survive. As Wilfred Cantwell Smith has recently written, "unless men can learn to understand and to be loyal to each other across religious frontiers, unless ... [men] can build a world in which people of profoundly different faiths can live together and work together, then the prospects for our planet's future are not bright[101]." In the present age of increasing religious encounter, recognition of religious human rights, both by governments and religions, is not only a moral imperative but also a practical necessity for the creation of a world community and possibly the survival of the human family.

---

[99] *The Pope Speaks*, 11:84-94.

[100] See Vatican II, "Declaration on the Relation of the Church to Non-Christian Religions," published in John Hick and Brian Hebblethwaite, eds. *Christiantiy and Other Religions* (Philadelphia: Fortress Press, 1980), 80-86.

[101] Wilfred Cantwell Smith, "The Christian in a Religiously Plural World," in ibid., 95.

CONCLUSION

The issue of religious human rights is one of growing significance in today's world. The growth of religious pluralism is worldwide and constitutes one of the major challenges facing all of the religions of the world today. The increasing presence of multiple faiths in secular societies makes religious isolation impossible and interfaith encounters inevitable. The worldwide distribution of communities of virtually all of the major religious traditions should exacerbate the concern of all religions for guarantees of religious liberty and the protection of the religious rights of their own adherents and thereby for religious minorities generally.

The particular plea of this lecture is that the call for the recognition of religious human rights in the world community needs to be sounded by the religions themselves as well as by instruments of national and international law. The international dimension of the major world religions holds the promise of effecting important gains not only for the advancement of religious human rights, but also for genuine interfaith dialogue and collaboration on behalf of religious freedom and the building of a world community. Freedom of religion and conscience is not only a moral imperative worthy of universal support of religions around the world, it also needs to be seen as essential for the creation of a world community and may well prove to be crucial in the survival of the human family.

It is to be fervently hoped that the words of the Charter of Paris for a New Europe, signed by thirty-four member nations of the Helsinki Final Act, in which religious freedom and other fundamental freedoms are made "the birthright of all human beings ... inalienable, guaranteed by law" may become realized throughout the world[102]. Grant that this expressed hope of the Charter of Paris will become an integral part of the work and witness of all churches and faiths everywhere.

---

[102] "Charter of Paris for a New Europe," A New Era of Democracy, Peace and Unity, 21 November 1990, 30 I.L.M. 193 (1990).

# PERSONALIA

CELESTINO MIGLIORE was born in Cuneo, Italy in 1952, where he was ordained a priest in 1977 after gaining a Licence in Theology at the Centre of Theological Studies in Fossano. He received a Doctorate in Canon Law at the Pontifical Lateran University, after which he was invited to continue his studies at the Pontifical Ecclesiastical Academy in Rome. He was sent in 1980 as Attaché to the Apostolic Delegation in Angola and in 1984 to the Apostolic Nunciature in the United States, where he was also Alternate Observer to the Organization of American States. In 1988 he was appointed to the Apostolic Nunciature in Egypt, remaining there for one year; he was then appointed Auditor at the Apostolic Nunciature in Warsaw, a post that he occupied until his appointment on 14 April 1992 as Special Envoy with the role of Permanent Observer of the Holy See to the Council of Europe. On 21 December 1995 he was appointed Undersecretary of the Section for Relations of States of the Secretariat of State. From 1996 he has been Visiting Professor at the Lateran University, where he teaches Ecclesiastical Diplomacy.

RIK TORFS was born in Turnhout, Belgium in 1956. He studied Law at Louvain University (lic. iur., 1979; lic. not., 1980) and Canon Law at Strasbourg and Louvain University (J.C.D., 1987). After one year of teaching at Utrecht University (The Netherlands), he became professor at the Faculty of Canon Law (K.U. Leuven) in 1988. Dean of the Faculty of Canon Law since 1993, R. Torfs published seven books and more than 150 articles on canon law, law, church and state relationships. He is editor of the *European Journal for Church and State Research*.

JAMES E. WOOD, JR. was born in Portsmouth, Virginia (U.S.A.) in 1922. He graduated from Carson-Newman College (B.A.), Colombia University (M.A.), and the Southern Baptist Theological Seminary (B.D., Th.M., Ph.D.). In addition, he received a diploma in Chinese Studies from Yale University and a Diploma in Japanese Studies from the Nagnuma School of Japanese Studies (Tokyo). In 1951, he was appointed Professor of Religion and Literature at Seinan Gakuin University (Japan), and joined the religion faculty of Baylor University in 1955, where he presently holds the position of Simon and Ethel Bunn Distinguished Professor of Church-State Studies. He holds honorary doctoral degrees in law (LL.D.) from Seinan Gakuin University (Japan) and Capital University Law School (U.S.A.) and the D.H.C. degree from Bucharest University (Romania). In 1983, he was a visiting scholar at Oxford University. Director of the J.M. Dawson Institute of Church-State Studies of Baylor University from the Institute's founding in 1958 and Founding Editor of *Journal of Church and State* in 1959, since June 1995 he has devoted his full time at Baylor University to teaching and research. He is the author/editor of twenty books, contributor to thirty-five additional volumes, and author of more than three hundred articles in numerous journals. President of the International Academy on Freedom of Religion and Belief since 1990, he has for many years been an active participant in international conferences and consultations on behalf of religious human rights in Africa, Asia, Europe, the Near East, North America, and Latin America.

# PUBLICATIES / PUBLICATIONS
## MSGR. W. ONCLIN CHAIR

Editor RIK TORFS

*Canon Law and Marriage. Monsignor W. Onclin Chair 1995*, **Leuven, Peeters, 1995, 36 p.**

R. TORFS, *The Faculty of Canon Law of K.U. Leuven in 1995*, 5-9.
C. BURKE, *Renewal, Personalism and Law*, 11-21.
R.G.W. HUYSMANS, *Enforcement and Deregulation in Canon Law*, 23-36.

*A Swing of the Pendulum. Canon Law in Modern Society. Monsignor W. Onclin Chair 1996*, **Leuven, Peeters, 1996, 64 p.**

R. TORFS, *Une messe est possible. Over de nabijheid van Kerk en geloof*, 7-11.
R. TORFS, *'Une messe est possible'. A Challenge for Canon Law*, 13-17.
J.M. SERRANO RUIZ, *Acerca del carácter personal del matrimonio: digresiones y retornos*, 19-31.
J.M. SERRANO RUIZ, *The Personal Character of Marriage. A Swing of the Pendulum*, 33-45.
F.G. MORRISEY, *Catholic Identity of Healthcare Institutions in a Time of Change*, 47-64.

*In Diversitate Unitas. Monsignor W. Onclin Chair 1997*, **Leuven, Peeters, 1997, 72 p.**

R. TORFS, *Pro Pontifice et Rege*, 7-13.
R. TORFS, *Pro Pontifice et Rege*, 15-22.
H. PREE, *The Divine and the Human of the Ius Divinum*, 23-41.
J.H. PROVOST, *Temporary Replacements or New Forms of Ministry: Lay Persons with Pastoral Care of Parishes*, 43-70.

*Bridging Past and Future. Monsignor W. Onclin Revisited. Monsignor W. Onclin Chair 1998*, **Leuven, Peeters, 1998, 87 p.**

P. CARD. LAGHI, *Message*, 7-9.
R. TORFS, *Kerkelijk recht in de branding. Terug naar monseigneur W. Onclin*, 11-20.
R. TORFS, *Canon Law in the Balance. Monsignor W. Onclin Revisited*, 21-31.
L. ÖRSY, *In the Service of the Holy Spirit: the Ecclesial Vocation of the Canon Lawyers*, 33-53.
P. COERTZEN, *Protection of Rights in the Church. A Reformed Perspective*, 55-87.

PRINTED ON PERMANENT PAPER • IMPRIME SUR PAPIER PERMANENT • GEDRUKT OP DUURZAAM PAPIER - ISO 9706

ORIENTALISTE, KLEIN DALENSTRAAT 42, B-3020 HERENT